Flash 5
Made Simple

Mike McGrath

Routledge
Taylor & Francis Group

LONDON AND NEW YORK

First published 2001 by Made Simple

2 Park Square, Milton Park, Abingdon, Oxon OX14 4RN
711 Third Avenue, New York, NY 10017, USA

Routledge is an imprint of the Taylor & Francis Group, an informa business

First issued in hardback 2017

British Library Cataloguing in Publication Data
A catalogue record for this book is available from the British Library

ISBN 978-0-7506-5361-9 (pbk)
ISBN 978-1-138-43622-0 (hbk)

Typeset by Mike McGrath
Icons designed by Sarah Ward © 1994
Transferred to digital printing 2006

FOR EVERY TITLE THAT WE PUBLISH, BUTTERWORTH-HEINEMANN
WILL PAY FOR BTCV TO PLANT AND CARE FOR A TREE.

Contents

Preface

Macromedia Flash is the application that is used to create those animated interactive multimedia pages you see on the Web. Designers love to use it because it allows them to efficiently produce and deliver Flash movies with stunning effects.

Virtually all modern web browsers can view Flash movies without needing any further software. This means that the same Flash movie can be viewed on any common web browser regardless of the operating system that is being used.

Flash can do much more than animate sound and vision though. Actions can be added to elements of a Flash movie to make them respond intelligently to the user. Flash 5 builds on earlier versions to provide more creative actions than ever before. This means that imaginative interaction can now make Flash movies a magical user experience.

This book is a beginner's guide to starting out with Flash 5 and assumes that the reader has no previous experience of working with vector graphics or animation programs. The Flash interface often provides several ways to perform a task but this book mostly concentrates on using the mouse pointer and gives the keyboard shortcuts for Flash on the Windows platform.

You are shown by example how to use the tools in the Flash interface to create and manipulate graphics before learning how to animate them. You will discover how to create rollover buttons that interact with the user and how to add sound to your movies so they really come alive. Finally the book explains a number of ways to deliver your movie for viewing.

After following the examples in this book you will be able to start creating your own exciting Flash movies.

Take note

This book uses some conventions for clarity:

Keyboard keys are shown inside square brackets, such as [Enter].

Steps through menus to sub menus are shown with the greater—than angle bracket, for instance File > Open.

1 Flash basics

Launching Flash

The Macromedia Flash installer will have created icons which can be used to launch the Flash interface.

A Flash interface displays these three major components:

- The Flash toolbar which provides menu commands that can be used as an alternative to using graphic controls or keyboard shortcuts

- The Flash toolbox which contains the creative tools

- The Flash editor where graphics and text are drawn

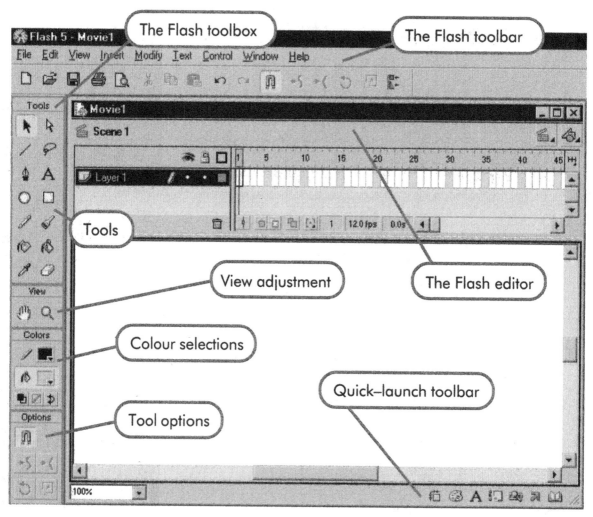

2

The Flash editor

The editor window is where Flash images and animations are created. A new editor window can be opened from the Flash toolbar by selecting the File > New menu options.

Each editor window has these three major components:

- A layers panel to create and manipulate drawing layers

- A timeline panel that has graduated markings and controls that are used to create animations

- A blank area that is called the 'stage' where all graphics are created in Flash.

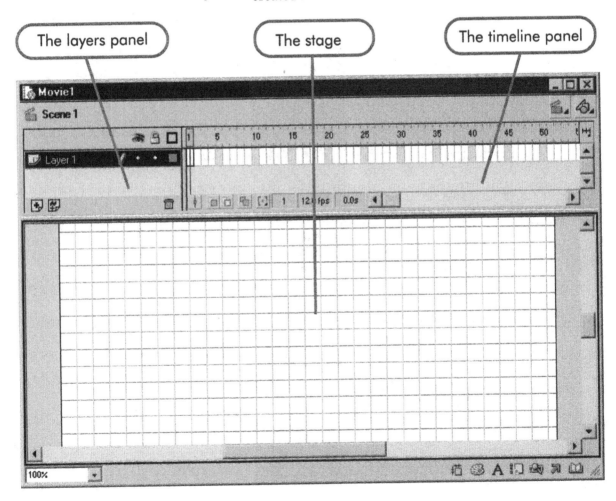

The Flash toolbox

The toolbox contains all the tools needed to draw, paint and manipulate images in the stage area of the Flash editor. Select a tool by clicking on any of the icons in the tools panel. Separate panels contain icons to select the view of the stage, the colours to draw or paint and further options that can be applied.

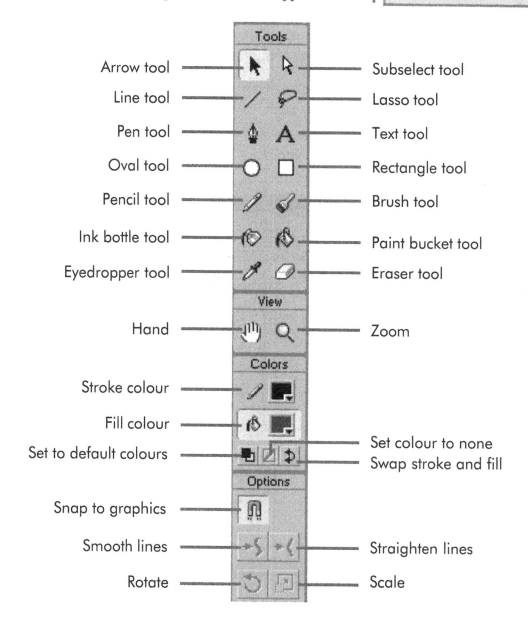

Arrow tool	Subselect tool
Line tool	Lasso tool
Pen tool	Text tool
Oval tool	Rectangle tool
Pencil tool	Brush tool
Ink bottle tool	Paint bucket tool
Eyedropper tool	Eraser tool
Hand	Zoom
Stroke colour	
Fill colour	
Set to default colours	Set colour to none / Swap stroke and fill
Snap to graphics	
Smooth lines	Straighten lines
Rotate	Scale

4

Drawing a shape

1 Select the oval tool by clicking it in the tool-box, or by pressing [O].
Or select the Rectangle tool by clicking it in the toolbox, or by pressing [R].

2 Click on the stage and hold down the mouse button.

3 Keep the mouse button pressed and drag the pointer across the stage.

4 Finally release the mouse button.

❏ Flash will draw the shape on the stage in the current colours.

Ovals and rectangle shapes can be easily drawn on the stage with the oval and rectangle tools. With a shape tool selected, just click on the stage and drag the mouse to see a preview of the shape appear. The size of the preview changes dynamically as the mouse is moved. Release the mouse button when the shape is the desired size and Flash will draw the final shape. The shape will have both an outline and a filled centre in the colours that are currently selected in the Colors panel on the toolbox.

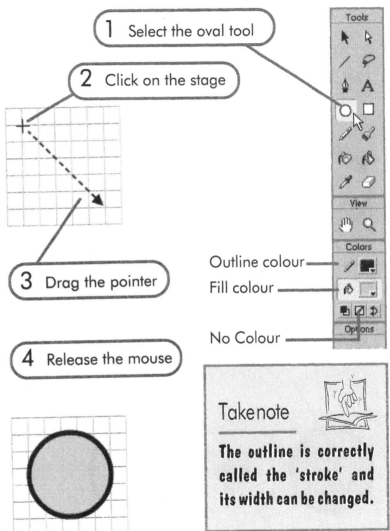

1 Select the oval tool

2 Click on the stage

3 Drag the pointer

4 Release the mouse

Outline colour
Fill colour
No Colour

Tip

Drag and hold [Shift] to draw a perfect circle.

Select the No Colour button to draw just an outline shape.

Take note

The outline is correctly called the 'stroke' and its width can be changed.

Selecting elements

Graphic shapes that are drawn on the Flash stage are made up of separate elements. A filled circle, for example, comprises a centre fill element and an outline stroke element. Elements can be manipulated to change their size, shape, colour or position.

The element that is to be manipulated must first be selected by the arrow tool to identify it to the program. Flash adds a highlight pattern to the selected element to make it recognisable to the user. The highlight pattern disappears when the element is deselected.

Basic steps

1 Select the arrow tool by clicking it in the Toolbox, or by pressing [V].

2 Click on the required element to select it.

3 Hold down the [Shift] then click the selected element to deselect it.

❏ The appearance of the element returns to normal once it has been deselected.

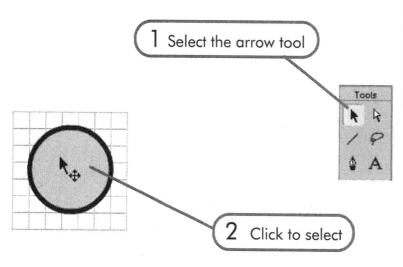

1 Select the arrow tool

2 Click to select

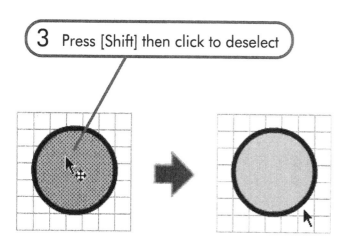

3 Press [Shift] then click to deselect

Take note

Notice that the cursor style changes when the pointer is positioned over an element.

The cursor resumes its normal style when the pointer returns to a blank area of the stage.

Basic steps

1 Select the arrow tool by clicking it in the toolbox or by pressing [V].

2 Click on an element to make a first selection.

3 Hold down [Shift] then click on other elements to make additional selections.

4 Click on a blank area of the stage to deselect all elements.

❑ The appearance of all selected elements returns to normal once they are deselected.

Selecting multiple elements

Several elements on the stage can be selected together in order to manipulate their features simultaneously.

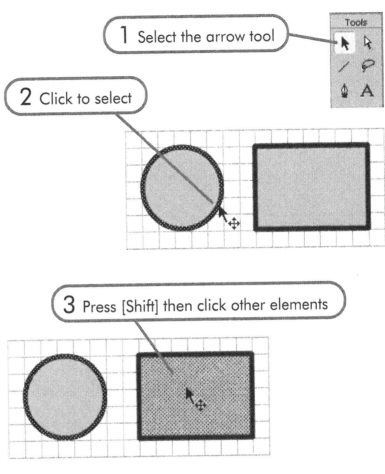

1 Select the arrow tool

2 Click to select

3 Press [Shift] then click other elements

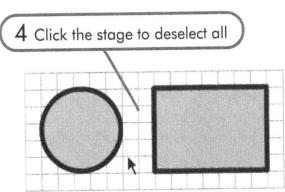

4 Click the stage to deselect all

Tip

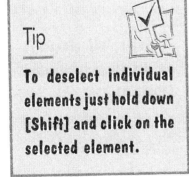

To deselect individual elements just hold down [Shift] and click on the selected element.

Boxing selections

An easy way to select multiple elements quickly is to drag the arrow tool across the stage to create a selection box area. All elements that are inside this box will be selected.

If the selection box encloses just a part of an element then that part which is inside the selection box will be selected.

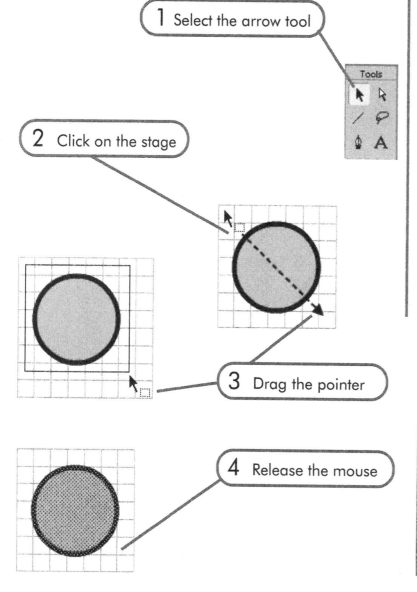

1 Select the arrow tool

2 Click on the stage

3 Drag the pointer

4 Release the mouse

1 Select the arrow tool by clicking it in the toolbox or press [V].

2 Click on the stage and hold down the mouse button.

3 Keep the mouse button pressed and drag the pointer across the stage.

❑ The selection box appears and will dynamically change as the mouse moves.

4 Finally release the mouse button.

❑ The box will disappear and all the enclosed elements are selected.

Tip

To select all elements on the stage just press [Ctrl+A].

[Delete] will remove selected elements.

Basic steps

1 Select the lasso tool by clicking it in the tool-box or by pressing [L].

2 Click on the polygon option in the toolbox.

3 Click on the stage to set the starting point of the selection area.

4 Click additional points to draw a selection area around a shape.

5 Finally double-click to draw a line back to the starting point and make the selection.

❑ The selection area lines will disappear leaving enclosed elements selected.

Tip

To select just a part of an element to work with draw around it with either the arrow tool or lasso tool .

Lassoing selections

Irregularly shaped selections can be made using the lasso tool. This allows freehand selection areas to be drawn on the stage by holding down the mouse button while drawing. Choosing the polygon option makes the lasso tool easier to use by drawing the selection area from point-to-point. Each click denotes a new point and a double-click completes the selection area.

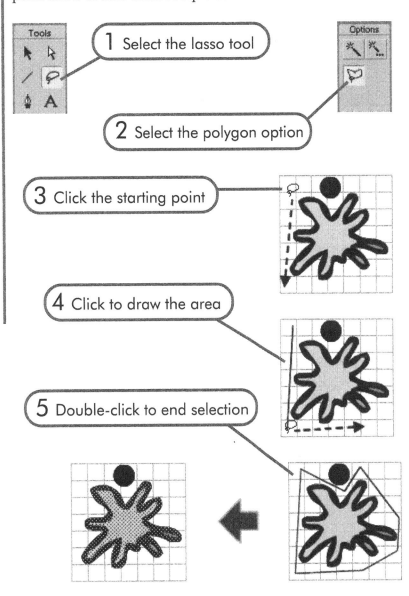

1 Select the lasso tool

2 Select the polygon option

3 Click the starting point

4 Click to draw the area

5 Double-click to end selection

Grouping elements

Graphic elements on the Flash stage can be grouped together so they can be treated as a single object. The entire grouped object can be repositioned, enlarged or reduced, and rotated. Grouped objects do not interact with other graphic elements on the stage. If a grouped object is positioned so that it overlaps other graphics or groups they will simply stack up on top of each other.

Flash displays a visible bounding box around a grouped object when it is selected, to identify it as a group. This box disappears when the group is deselected.

1 Select all the elements to be grouped – using any of the selection methods described earlier in this chapter.

2 Press [Ctrl+G] to create the group and see the bounding box appear.

3 Press [Ctrl+B] to break the group apart – notice the bounding box disappear.

4 Click on a blank area of the stage to deselect all elements.

❑ The elements are now back in their original state and can be individually edited.

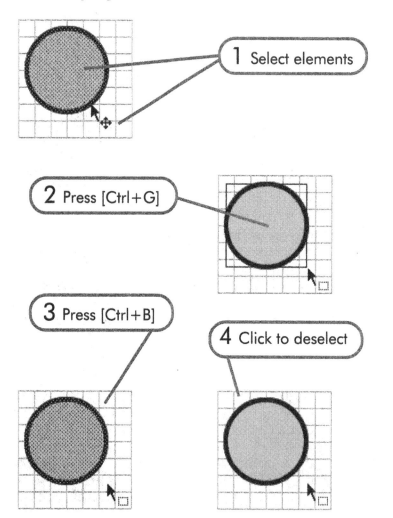

1 Select elements

2 Press [Ctrl+G]

3 Press [Ctrl+B]

4 Click to deselect

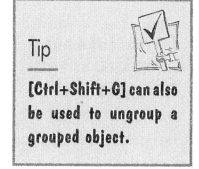

Tip

[Ctrl+Shift+G] can also be used to ungroup a grouped object.

Basic steps

1 Right-click on a group
   to open the group
   context menu.

2 Click the edit selected
   menu item to enter
   into editing mode.

3 Select the elements to
   be edited as normal.

4 Double-click a blank
   area of the stage to
   leave editing mode.

❑ The stage returns to
   standard mode and
   all dimmed graphics
   resume their usual
   appearance.

Editing Groups

Flash provides a special editing mode that can be used on
elements in a group. A click of the right mouse button over a
grouped object will open a context menu from which 'Edit
Selected' will put the stage into editing mode. Elements in the
Group can then be edited as normal and all other graphics on the
stage are dimmed to avoid confusion.

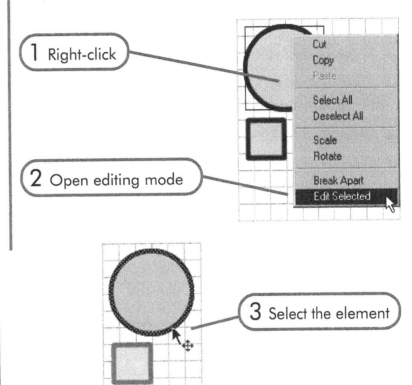

1 Right-click

2 Open editing mode

3 Select the element

4 Double-click the stage

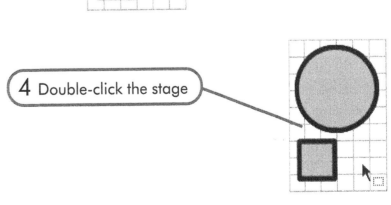

Summary

❑ The Flash toolbar provides menu commands that can be used as an alternative to using graphic controls or keyboard shortcuts.

❑ The Flash interface has a main window containing the Flash editor and the Flash toolbox.

❑ The Flash editor consists of the stage area, the layer panel and the timeline panel.

❑ Images are created on the stage in the Flash editor.

❑ All tools needed to draw, paint and manipulate images on the stage are contained in the toolbox.

❑ Graphics may consist of stroke and fill colours.

❑ Circles and ovals can be drawn on the stage using the oval tool.

❑ Squares and rectangles can be drawn on the stage using the rectangle tool.

❑ The arrow tool can be used to select elements to work with on the stage.

❑ The arrow tool can select several elements at once by dragging a box around them.

❑ The lasso tool can select several elements at once by drawing a selection area around them.

❑ Elements can be combined in a single group object that can be moved, re-sized or rotated.

❑ Elements in a group can be edited using the special editing mode.

2 Drawing in Flash

Choosing colours

The colours to draw on the stage can be set for both the stroke and fill using the toolbox Colors panel. Clicking on either of the coloured blocks in this panel produces a dialog box containing a swatch of colours to choose from. When a colour is chosen the dialog box closes and the Colors panel displays the current colours that will be used when drawing on the stage.

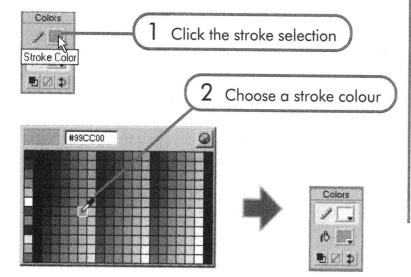

1   Click the stroke selection

2   Choose a stroke colour

3   Click the fill selection

4   Choose a fill colour

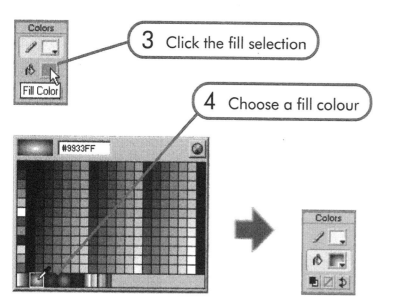

Basic steps

1   Click on the top colour block that shows the current stroke colour.

2   Click on the desired new stroke colour from the swatch.

3   Click on the bottom colour block showing the current fill colour.

4   Click on the desired new fill colour from the swatch.

❏   The newly selected colours are displayed in the Colors panel.

Take note

The swatch dialog box has additional choices at the bottom. These offer a variety of gradient coloured fills.

The pointer changes to an Eyedropper whenever a colour can be chosen.

14

Basic steps

1 Click the mixer button to open its dialog box.

2 Click on the fill or stroke icon to choose which one to set.

3 Click on the multicoloured panel to specify the desired colour.

4 Click the X button to close the dialog box.

❑ The newly selected colour is displayed in the Colors panel.

Mixing more colours

Colours which are not available in the standard swatch can be specified in the mixer dialog box. This is launched from the small toolbar at the bottom right-hand corner of the editor window and has a duplicate of the toolbox Color panel features. The mixer dialog box also contains a multi-coloured panel that can be clicked to specify an exact colour at the point where it is clicked.

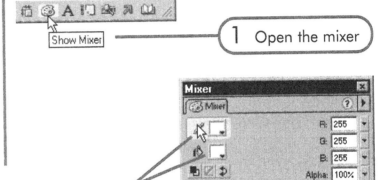

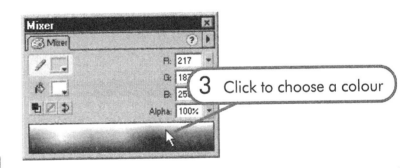

Tip

Alternatively set the RGB and Alpha values to specify a colour.

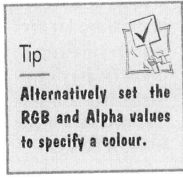

Drawing lines

Straight lines can be drawn on the stage using the line tool in the Flash toolbox. It is important to note that lines are purely stroke elements and do not have any fill component. The line style, colour and thickness can be specified using the stroke options. These are part of the info dialog box that can be launched from the toolbar at the bottom right-hand corner of the editor.

1 Click on the line tool icon in the toolbox or press [N].

2 Click the button to open the info dialog.

3 Click the stroke tab.

4 Click the drop-down button and choose a line style.

5 Click the slider button and adjust to the required thickness.

❑ A preview of how the line will appear is shown in the panel at the bottom of the stroke dialog box.

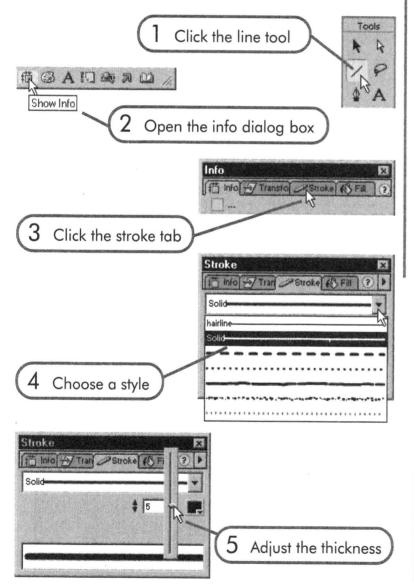

1 Click the line tool

Show Info

2 Open the info dialog box

3 Click the stroke tab

4 Choose a style

5 Adjust the thickness

Tip

A colour block in the stroke dialog box displays the current stroke colour. You can click on this to open a swatch and choose a new stroke colour for the line.

Draw a line on the stage

Basic steps

1 Click on the line tool icon in the toolbox.

2 Move the pointer across the stage to the position where the line is to start.

3 Click and hold down the mouse button then drag the pointer to the position where the line is to end. A preview of the line is displayed on the stage.

4 Release the mouse button when the line preview is the desired length and position.

❑ A line is drawn in the current stroke colour, style and thickness.

The line tool is used to draw a line on the stage. An initial click on the mouse button sets the starting point then the mouse can be dragged to the finishing point. The line is not actually drawn until the mouse button is released.

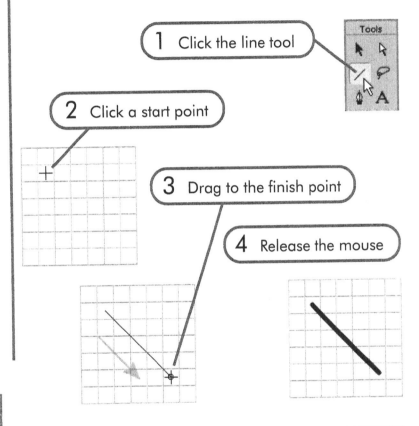

1 Click the line tool

2 Click a start point

3 Drag to the finish point

4 Release the mouse

Tip

Hold down [shift] while dragging a line to keep it strictly horizontal, vertical or at an angle of 45 degrees.

Take note

At any time you can undo previous drawing actions by clicking the Undo button on the toolbar, or by pressing [Ctrl+Z], as many times as needed.

Pencil drawing

Freehand lines can be drawn on the stage using the pencil tool in the Flash toolbox. Lines will be drawn in the style, colour and thickness of the current stroke. When the pencil tool is selected a button appears in the toolbox options panel that can be clicked to offer three drawing modes. Drawing on the stage in ink mode leaves all the usual jagged edges that appear in freehand drawing. The appearance of these lines is greatly enhanced if the smooth mode is used instead to remove the imperfections.

Basic steps

1 Click on the pencil tool icon in the tool-box or press [Y].

2 Click the button in the options panel to display the modes.

3 Click on the smooth mode option.

4 Click and drag to draw a preview line on the stage.

5 Release the mouse button at the end position of the line.

❑ A line is drawn in the current stroke colour, style and thickness and jagged edges are smoothed out.

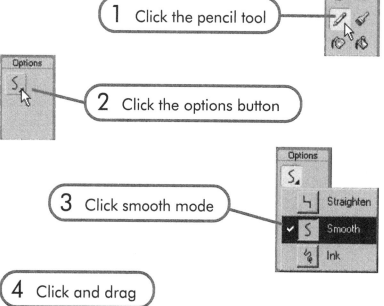

1 Click the pencil tool

2 Click the options button

3 Click smooth mode

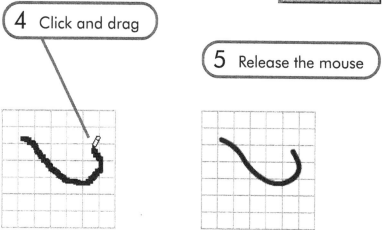

4 Click and drag

5 Release the mouse

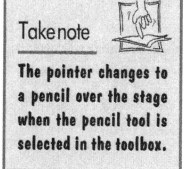

Take note

The pointer changes to a pencil over the stage when the pencil tool is selected in the toolbox.

Basic steps

1 Click on the pencil tool icon in the tool-box or press [Y].

2 Click the button in the options panel to display the modes.

3 Click on the straighten mode option.

4 Click and drag to draw a preview line on the stage.

5 Release the mouse button at the end position of the line.

❑ A line is drawn in the current stroke colour, style and thickness and jagged edges are straightened out.

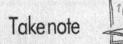
Straightening pencil lines

The straighten mode option that is available when the pencil tool is selected provides an easy way to refine freehand lines with jagged edges into straight lines or regular arcs. Additionally this is an intelligent function that automatically evaluates the drawn line to see if it is close to being a rectangle or oval shape. If so, Flash will transform the freehand drawn line into a rectangle or oval of the same approximate dimensions and with the current stroke settings.

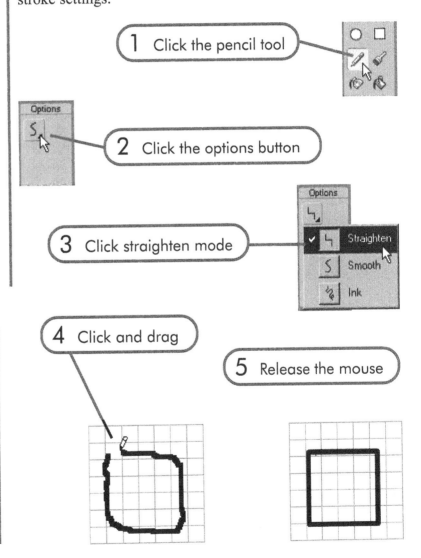

1 Click the pencil tool

2 Click the options button

3 Click straighten mode

4 Click and drag

5 Release the mouse

19

Changing lines

The arrow tool that is used to select elements can also be used to modify lines. Placing the arrow tool at the end of a line causes the cursor to change and allows the end point of the line to be dragged to a new position. Similarly placing the cursor along a line's length enables the line to be dragged into a curve.

1 Click on the line tool icon in the toolbox or press [N].

2 Click on the stage and drag the mouse to draw a line.

3 Click on the arrow tool icon in the tool-box or press [V].

4 Click on the end of the line and drag the mouse to reposition the line's end point.

5 Click on the line's length and drag the mouse to bend the line into a curve.

❑ When the mouse is released the line is drawn with its new position and shape.

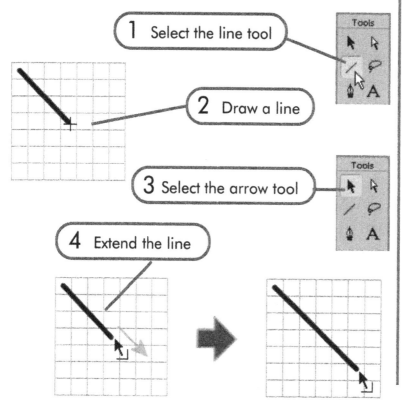

1 Select the line tool

2 Draw a line

3 Select the arrow tool

4 Extend the line

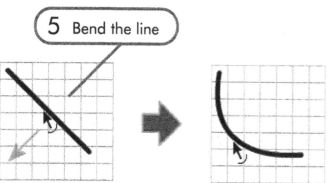

5 Bend the line

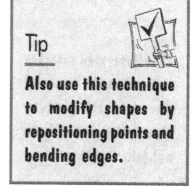

Tip

Also use this technique to modify shapes by repositioning points and bending edges.

Modify an existing line

Basic steps

1 Select the line with the arrow tool by clicking on it.

2 Keep the mouse button pressed down and drag the line to a new location.

3 Click on the button at the bottom of the editor window to open the info window.

4 Click on the stroke tab to display the current stroke settings.

5 Click on the style button then pick a style from the drop down menu.

6 Click the colour block then choose a colour from the swatch.

7 Click the size button then use the slider to set the line thickness.

8 Click on the stage to deselect the line.

❑ When deselected the line will have the new stroke specifications.

A selected existing line can be repositioned using the arrow tool and its appearance can be modified by changing the current stroke specifications to alter its colour, style and thickness.

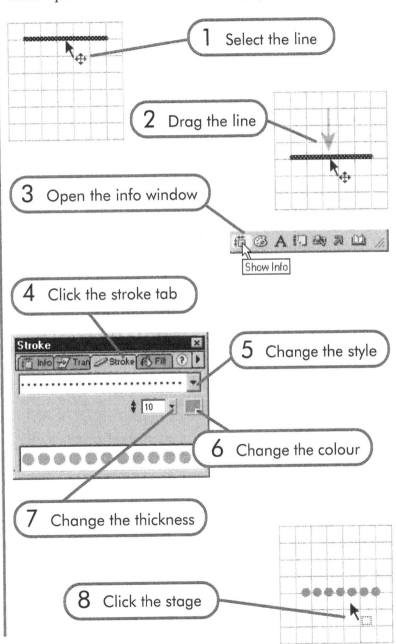

1 Select the line

2 Drag the line

3 Open the info window

Show Info

4 Click the stroke tab

5 Change the style

6 Change the colour

7 Change the thickness

8 Click the stage

Drawing curves

The pen tool draws by creating a series of points that are joined together to form a line. A simple click on the stage with the pen tool adds a point to the line series. A click and drag adds a point that has adjustable features called bézier handles which allow the line from a previous point to be curved.

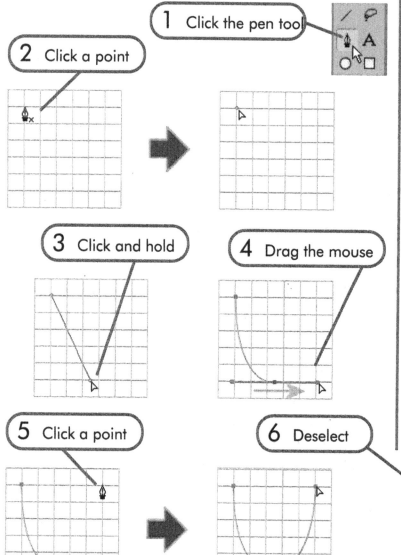

Basic steps

1 Select the pen tool by clicking the icon or by pressing [P].

2 Click on the stage to set a first point.

3 Click on the stage at a second point and keep the mouse button pressed down – a straight preview line to the first point appears.

4 Drag the mouse to curve the preview line to the first point.

5 Click on the stage to add another point – the preview line joins to the previous point continuing the curve.

6 Click another tool or press [Ctrl+Shift+A] to deselect the line.

❑ When deselected the finished line is drawn.

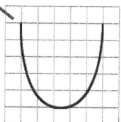

Basic steps

1 Click the icon or press [A] to use the subselect tool.

2 Click on a line to select it.

3 Click a point to reveal its bézier handles.

4 Click and drag the handle to change the curve of the line.

5 Click on a point to select it.

6 Drag the point to change its position.

7 Click another tool or press [Ctrl+Shift+A] to deselect the line.

❑ When deselected the finished line is drawn.

Tip ✓

Click a selected line with the pen tool to add a point.

Select a point then press [Delete] to remove it.

Changing curves

The subselect tool in the toolbox can be used to modify existing lines. When a line is selected with the subselect tool that line reverts to its preview state. Points and bézier handles can then be adjusted to change the shape of the line.

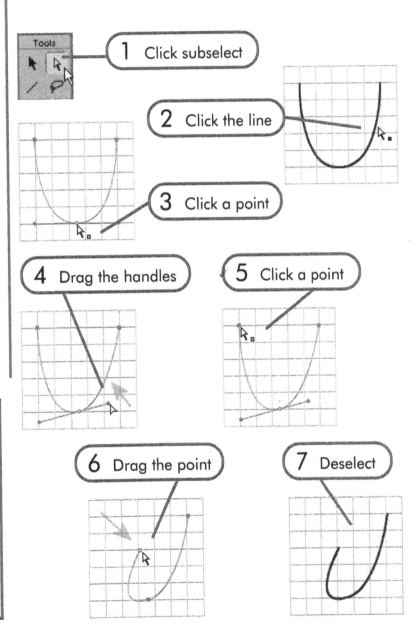

1 Click subselect

2 Click the line

3 Click a point

4 Drag the handles

5 Click a point

6 Drag the point

7 Deselect

Summary

❑ Stroke and fill colours can be picked from the swatch that appears when you click either of the colour blocks in the toolbox Colors panel.

❑ More colours are available in the mixer dialog box.

❑ The mixer and stroke dialogs can be opened from the toolbar at the bottom of the editor window.

❑ Stroke style, colour and thickness can be specified in the stroke dialog box.

❑ The line tool is used to draw straight lines.

❑ The pencil tool is used to draw freehand lines.

❑ The pencil tool has useful option modes to smooth or straighten the lines that it draws.

❑ The arrow tool can be used to bend existing lines and reposition their end points.

❑ Existing lines can also be modified by redefining their stroke settings in the stroke window.

❑ The pen tool can draw lines by creating a series of points to be joined together.

❑ Bézier handles can bend the lines between points.

❑ The subselect tool can be used to adjust the points and handles in an existing line.

3 Painting in Flash

Filling with colour

Lines that have been drawn into joined-up shapes can be filled with colour using the paint bucket tool. The shape will be filled with the currently selected fill colour that is displayed in the fill colour block of the toolbox Color panel.

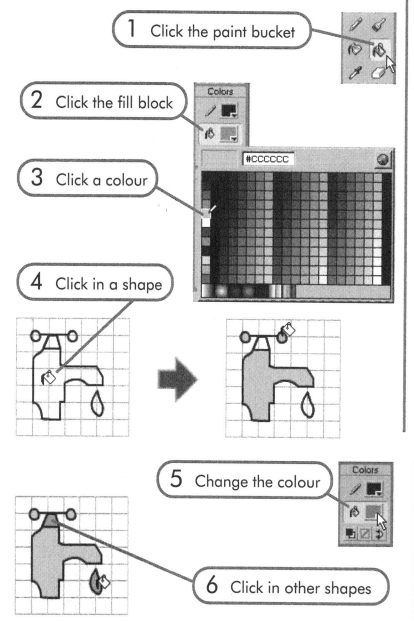

1 Click the paint bucket

2 Click the fill block

#CCCCCC

3 Click a colour

4 Click in a shape

5 Change the colour

6 Click in other shapes

Basic steps

1 Click on the paint bucket tool icon or press [K].

2 Click on the fill colour block in the Colors panel to open the swatch dialog box.

3 Click on a colour to set the new fill colour.

4 Click inside a shape to fill with the selected colour.

5 Click on the fill colour block and choose another colour from the swatch.

6 Click inside shapes to fill each with a newly selected fill colour.

❑ The paint bucket fills each shape with the current fill colour.

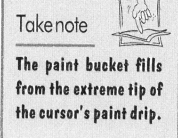

Take note

The paint bucket fills from the extreme tip of the cursor's paint drip.

Basic steps

1 Click the paint bucket icon or press [K].

2 Click the gaps button in the options panel.

3 Click on the required gap setting.

4 Click on the shape to attempt to fill it.

5 If necessary zoom out – click the zoom tool or press [Z].

6 Click on zoom out (–) then click on the stage to zoom to 50%.

7 Reselect the paint bucket tool and try again to apply the fill.

8 Finally zoom in (+) to return to 100% size.

❑ The shape will be filled across the gap.

Take note

This example illustrates a gradient colour fill — see the note on page 14.

Changing fills

A shape that has been drawn freehand on the stage may have small gaps between lines so that the shape is not exactly joined. Flash can still fill this shape using the paint bucket gap options. These allow you to specify the size of permissible gap when attempting to apply a fill with the paint bucket tool. If the gap is too big the fill will not be applied. Often this can be overcome by zooming out to temporarily reduce the physical gap size.

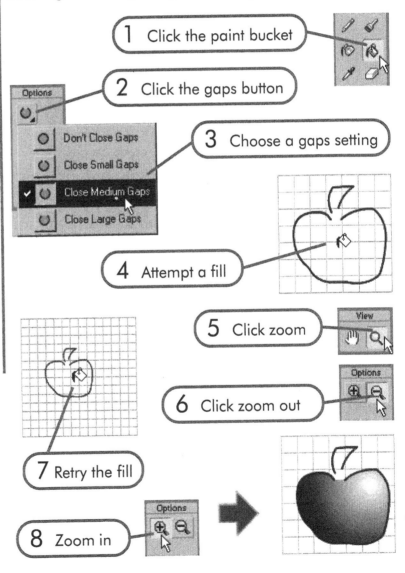

1 Click the paint bucket

2 Click the gaps button

Options

Don't Close Gaps
Close Small Gaps
✓ Close Medium Gaps
Close Large Gaps

3 Choose a gaps setting

4 Attempt a fill

5 Click zoom

6 Click zoom out

7 Retry the fill

8 Zoom in

Brushing colour

The Flash brush tool provides a means to paint freehand strokes of colour on the stage. It is important to note that these brush strokes are purely fill elements and do not have any stroke component. The brush size and shape can be specified using the brush options which are displayed in the toolbox options panel when the brush tool is selected.

1   Click on the brush tool icon in the toolbox or press [B].

2   Click the paint modes button in the options panel to display the paint mode options.

3   Click on the paint normal option to use the brush normally.

4   Click on the size button to display a menu of brush sizes.

5   Click on the desired brush size to select it.

6   Click on the shape button to display a menu of available brush shapes.

7   Click on the desired brush shape to select it to paint with.

☐   The brush tool is now ready to paint in its normal mode using the specified size and shape of brush.

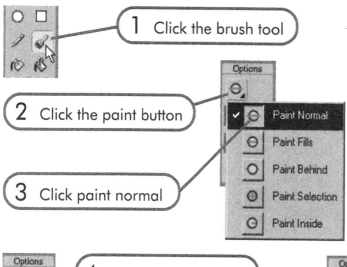

1   Click the brush tool

2   Click the paint button

3   Click paint normal

Options

Paint Normal
Paint Fills
Paint Behind
Paint Selection
Paint Inside

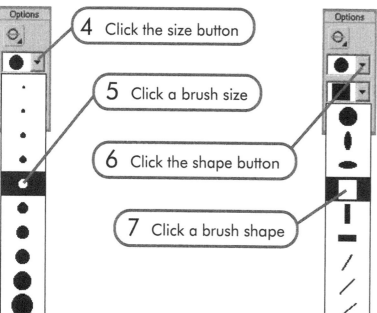

4   Click the size button

5   Click a brush size

6   Click the shape button

7   Click a brush shape

Basic steps

1   Click on the brush tool or press [B].

2   Set the desired colour, brush size and shape.

3   Click on the stage and hold down the mouse button.

4   Drag the mouse to paint a brush stroke.

5   Change the colour, brush size and shape.

6   Click on the stage and hold down the mouse button.

7   Drag the mouse to paint another brush stroke.

❑   The second brush stroke is painted on top of the first one.

Tip

Holding down [Shift] when painting restricts the brush strokes to horizontal or vertical.

Using the brush

To paint with the brush tool just click on the stage and drag the mouse to create a brush stroke. The brush will paint using the current fill colour, paint mode, brush size and brush shape.

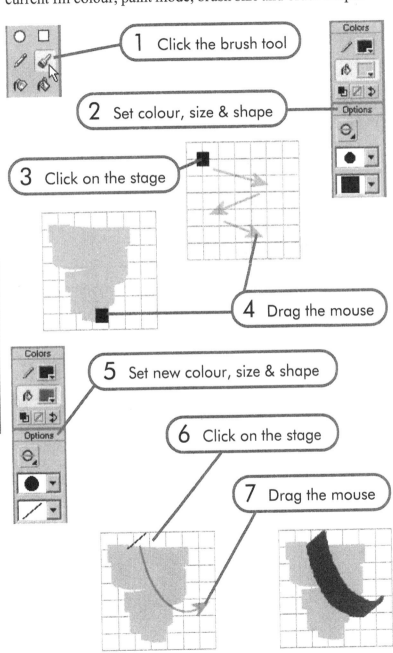

1   Click the brush tool

2   Set colour, size & shape

3   Click on the stage

4   Drag the mouse

5   Set new colour, size & shape

6   Click on the stage

7   Drag the mouse

Selective painting

The brush tool has some useful options that allow painting to be confined to selected parts of the stage or existing graphic. These options are available from the menu that is displayed by clicking the paint button in the toolbox options panel. The paint behind mode allows painting behind an existing graphic.

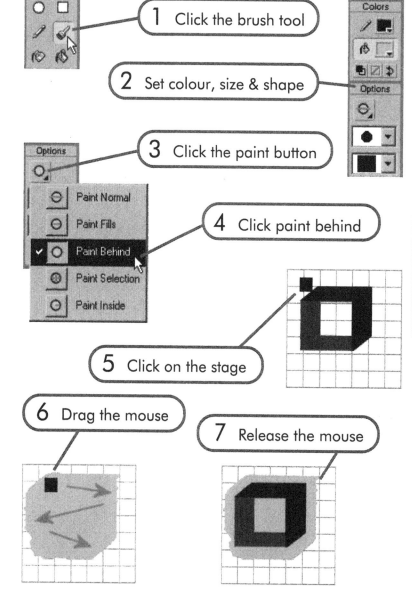

1 Click the brush tool

2 Set colour, size & shape

3 Click the paint button

4 Click paint behind

5 Click on the stage

6 Drag the mouse

7 Release the mouse

Basic steps

1 Click on the brush tool or press [B].

2 Set the desired colour, brush size and shape.

3 Click on the paint button in the options panel to display the paint modes menu.

4 Click on the paint behind mode.

5 Click on the stage at the starting point.

6 Drag the mouse over the initial graphic to paint on the stage.

7 Release the mouse button to stop painting and reveal the graphic in front of the paint.

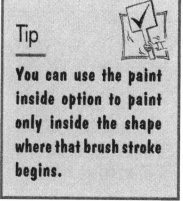

Tip

You can use the paint inside option to paint only inside the shape where that brush stroke begins.

Basic steps

1 Click on the rectangle tool icon or press [R].

2 Click the no colour button so that no stroke will be applied.

3 Click and drag on the stage to draw a first rectangle.

4 Click and drag on the stage to draw another rectangle overlapping the first one.

5 Click on the ink bottle tool or press [S].

6 Change the stroke colour from the no colour setting to a desired colour.

7 Click anywhere on these overlapping rectangles.

❑ The ink bottle tool creates a stroke out-line around the com-bined rectangles using the current stroke settings for colour, thickness and style.

Overlapping unstroked fill shapes can be combined into a single shape by adding an overall stroke with the ink bottle tool. This can create interesting possibilities when designing in Flash. Unstroked fill shapes can be added to the stage using the rectangle tool or oval tool with the current Stroke set to have no colour. The ink bottle tool can then apply a uniform stroke around the overlapping fill shapes in just a single action.

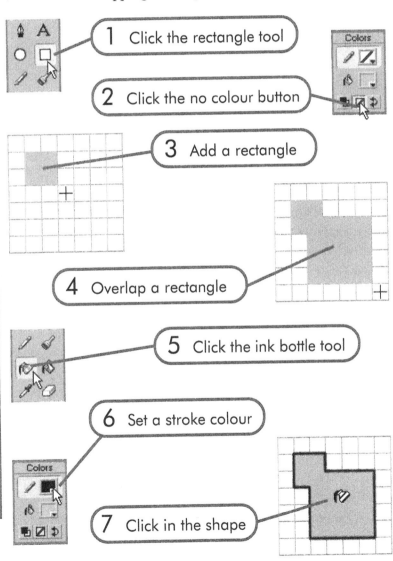

1 Click the rectangle tool

2 Click the no colour button

3 Add a rectangle

4 Overlap a rectangle

5 Click the ink bottle tool

6 Set a stroke colour

7 Click in the shape

Erasing graphics

The eraser tool is used to erase graphics from the stage and works in a similar manner to the brush tool. The eraser has mode options that mirror those of the brush tool and are used in the same way. When the eraser tool is used in its normal mode it erases from the stage all lines and fills that it passes over.

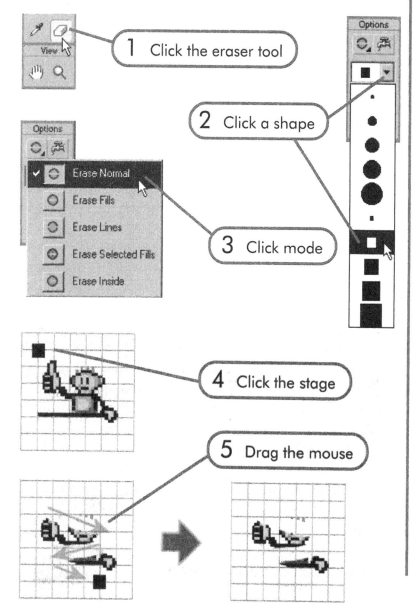

1 Click the eraser tool

2 Click a shape

3 Click mode

4 Click the stage

5 Drag the mouse

1 Click on the eraser tool icon or press [E].

2 Click on the shape button then choose the eraser size and shape from the menu.

3 Click the eraser modes button then click on the erase normal option.

4 Click on the stage at the starting point.

5 Keep the mouse button pressed down and rub the mouse from side to side like you would with a real eraser.

❑ All parts of the lines and fills that are in the path of the eraser tool are now removed.

❑ If you have accidentally erased a graphic you can undo the eraser operation by clicking Edit > Undo on the toolbar, or just by pressing [Ctrl+Z].

Basic steps

1 Use the arrow tool or other selection method to select the elements that are to be erased.

2 Click on the eraser tool icon or press [E].

3 Click the eraser modes button then click on the erase normal option.

4 Click on the faucet mode button in the options panel.

5 Click on any of the selected elements.

❑ All elements that were selected are erased from the stage.

Using the Eraser Faucet

Elements on the stage can be removed with just a single click using the eraser faucet mode. This mode is selected by clicking the faucet (tap) icon when the Eraser tool is selected. When the Eraser tool is using Faucet mode the cursor changes to look like a dripping tap. Simply click on any single element to erase it. Select a number of elements then click on any of the selections to erase them all from the stage at one go.

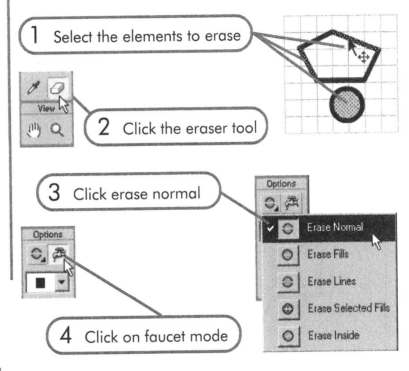

1 Select the elements to erase

2 Click the eraser tool

3 Click erase normal

4 Click on faucet mode

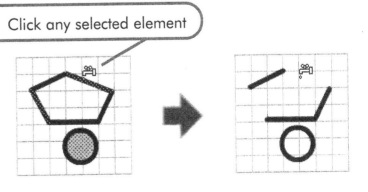

5 Click any selected element

Working with shapes

The arrow tool that is used to select elements can also be used to modify shapes. Placing the arrow tool at the corner of a shape causes the cursor to change and allows the corner to be dragged to a new position. Similarly placing the arrow tool along the edge of a shape enables that edge to be dragged into a curve.

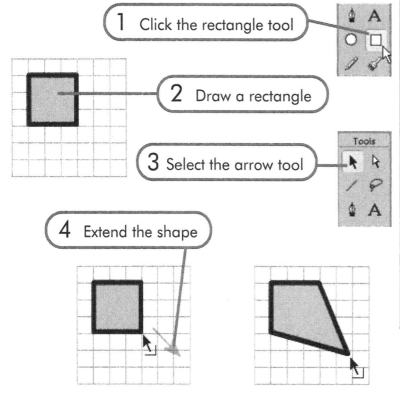

1   Click the rectangle tool

2   Draw a rectangle

3   Select the arrow tool

4   Extend the shape

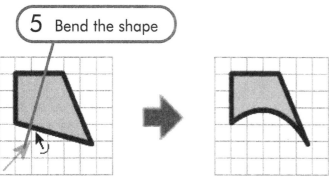

5   Bend the shape

Basic steps

1   Click on the rectangle tool icon or press [R].

2   Click on the stage and drag the mouse to draw a rectangle.

3   Click the arrow tool or press [V].

4   Click on a corner of the shape and drag the mouse to reposition that corner.

5   Click on an edge of the shape and drag the mouse to bend that edge.

☐   The rectangle shape is modified with a new corner position and a reshaped edge.

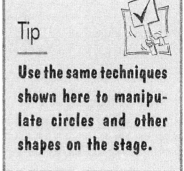

Tip

Use the same techniques shown here to manipulate circles and other shapes on the stage.

Basic steps

1 Click on the arrow tool icon or press [V].

2 Select the shape that is to be modified.

3 Click the rotate button in the options panel.

4 Click on a corner handle then drag the mouse to reposition that corner and so rotate the shape.

5 Click the scale button in the options panel.

6 Click on a corner handle then drag the mouse to reposition that corner and so resize the shape.

❑ The shape now has a modified size and orientation.

Tip

Drag a middle handle with either modifier to skew the shape.

Scaling and rotating shapes

The Arrow tool that is used to select elements also provides modifier options that can be used to rotate and resize shapes. When these are used a selected shape gains handles that can be grabbed by the cursor then dragged to modify it.

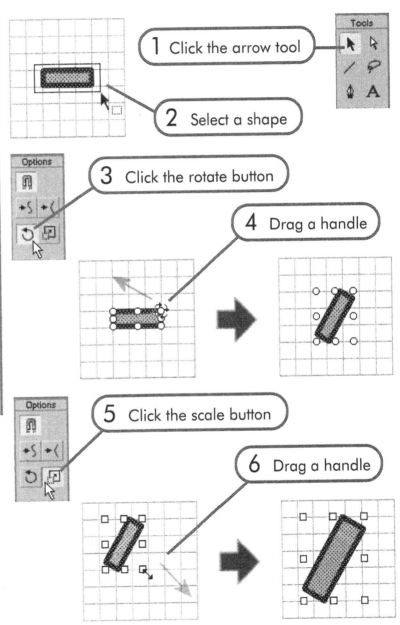

1 Click the arrow tool

2 Select a shape

3 Click the rotate button

4 Drag a handle

5 Click the scale button

6 Drag a handle

Moving shapes

Both fills and strokes contained in a shape, or a number of shapes, can be repositioned on the stage using the arrow tool. The elements that are to be moved should first be selected. When the arrow tool is positioned over selected elements the cursor changes to denote that the element can be grabbed by the mouse. Any selected element can then be dragged to reposition all selected elements on the stage. A preview of the new positions is shown until the mouse button is released when the elements are redrawn at those new locations.

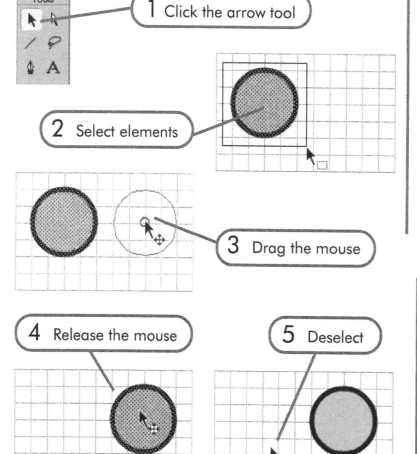

1 Click the arrow tool

2 Select elements

3 Drag the mouse

4 Release the mouse

5 Deselect

1 Click on the arrow tool icon or press [V].

2 Select the elements that are to be moved.

3 Click on any selected element and drag the mouse to reposition all the selected elements.

4 Release the mouse button when the preview appears at the desired location.

5 Click on the stage in a blank area to deselect all selected elements.

❑ All the strokes and fills that were selected are now redrawn at their new locations.

Tip

A single element does not need to be selected before it is moved — just click and drag with the arrow tool.

Basic steps

1 Click on the arrow tool icon or press [V].

2 Select the elements that are to be copied.

3 Click on the selection then hold down [Ctrl] while dragging the mouse.

4 Release the mouse button to make a preview copy of the selection appear.

5 Now release [Ctrl] and click on a blank area of the stage to deselect.

❏ A copy of the selection is drawn on the stage at the new location.

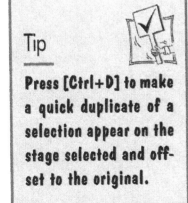

Tip

Press [Ctrl+D] to make a quick duplicate of a selection appear on the stage selected and offset to the original.

Copying shapes

Flash offers a number of ways to duplicate selected elements easily. Press [Ctrl+C] to copy a selection to the clipboard and then press [Ctrl+V] to paste a copy at the centre of the stage. Alternatively the clipboard selection can be pasted at the precise original location using [Ctrl+Shift+V]. This is very useful when making frames for animation.

To make a quick copy of any selected elements just hold down [Ctrl] then click and drag the selection.

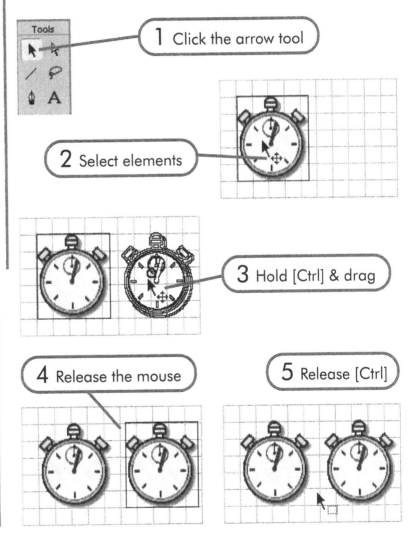

1 Click the arrow tool

2 Select elements

3 Hold [Ctrl] & drag

4 Release the mouse

5 Release [Ctrl]

Summary

- ❏ The paint bucket tool is used to fill shapes with the currently selected fill colour.

- ❏ Paint bucket options can be set to allow for gaps that may exist in a shape that is to be filled.

- ❏ Freehand brush strokes of fill colour can be painted on the stage using the brush tool.

- ❏ Brush tool options can specify selected parts of the stage or graphic to be painted.

- ❏ The ink bottle tool can add Stroke outlines to unstroked fill elements.

- ❏ The eraser tool removes all parts of strokes and fills that it passes over.

- ❏ Elements can be removed from the stage with a single click using the eraser tool in faucet mode.

- ❏ The arrow tool can be used to reposition corner points of a shape or to bend its edges.

- ❏ Arrow tool options allow shapes to be rotated, resized or skewed.

- ❏ Graphics can be repositioned on the stage by dragging them with the arrow tool.

- ❏ Holding down [Ctrl] while dragging will create a copy of that graphic.

4 Writing in Flash

Adding text

When the text tool has been selected in the toolbox just click a starting point on the stage then start typing to add some text. The text will appear on the stage in a single line text box that grows as the length of the text increases. This text box has a round handle at its top right hand corner that can be used to resize the box and so wrap the text contents to appear on multiple lines. The round handle then changes to a square handle to indicate that word wrap is turned on in that text box.

1 Click on the text tool or press [T].

2 Click on the stage at the point from which to start the text.

3 Start typing text – the text box will expand.

4 Click on the round handle and drag it to resize the text box.

5 Continue typing and now see the text wrap to the next line.

6 Select another tool or click on a blank area of the stage to deselect the text box.

☐ The text is added to the stage as a single graphic element.

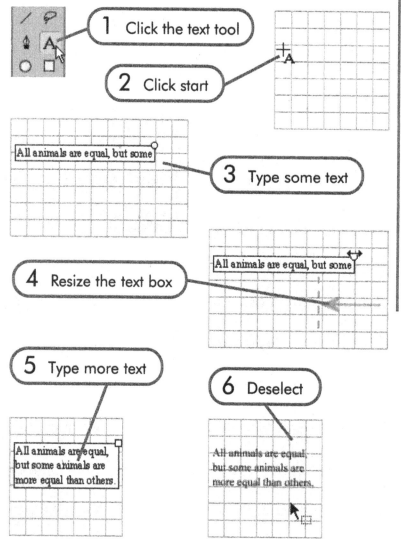

1 Click the text tool

2 Click start

3 Type some text

All animals are equal, but some

4 Resize the text box

All animals are equal, but some

5 Type more text

All animals are equal, but some animals are more equal than others.

6 Deselect

All animals are equal, but some animals are more equal than others.

Take note

The finished text block can be resized, rotated and repositioned with the arrow tool.

40

Changing text attributes

1 Click on the text tool or press [T].

2 Click and drag the mouse across the text to highlight it.

3 Click the button on the toolbar to launch the character dialog box or press [Ctrl+T].

4 Click on the font button then choose a font from the pop up menu that appears.

5 Click on the colours button then choose a different colour from the pop up swatch that appears.

6 Click on the height button then set the text height by adjusting the pop up slider that appears.

7 Click on the stage to deselect the text.

❑ The text is now re-drawn using the newly specified font, colour and height.

The font, text height and colour can be specified using the character window that is available from the toolbar at the bottom right hand corner of the editor. Select existing text and change these settings to alter the text appearance.

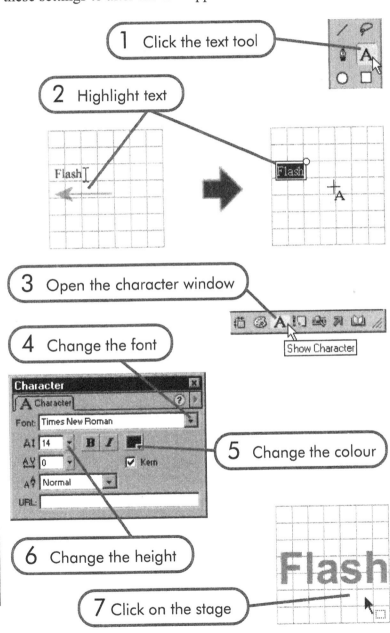

1 Click the text tool

2 Highlight text

3 Open the character window

4 Change the font

5 Change the colour

6 Change the height

7 Click on the stage

Changing text style

The style of text characters can be adjusted for spacing and set to bold or italic using the character window that is available from the toolbar at the bottom right-hand corner of the editor. Select existing text and change these settings to alter its style.

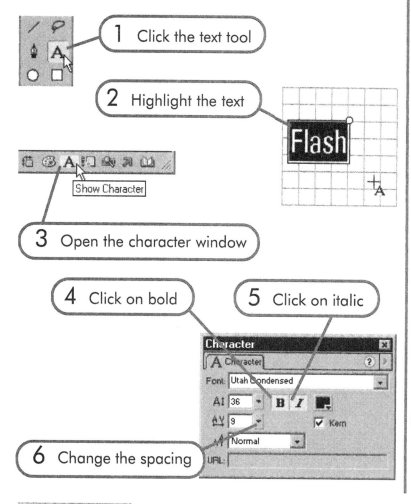

1 Click the text tool

2 Highlight the text

Show Character

3 Open the character window

4 Click on bold

5 Click on italic

Character
A Character
Font: Utah Condensed
A↕ 36 • B *I*
AV 9 • ✓ Kern
Normal •
URL

6 Change the spacing

7 Click on the stage

Flash

1 Click on the text tool or press [T].

2 Click and drag the mouse across the text to highlight it.

3 Click the button on the toolbar to launch the character window or press [Ctrl+T].

4 Click on the bold button.

5 Click on the italic button.

6 Click on the spacing button then adjust the pop up slider to change the space between characters.

7 Click on the stage to deselect the text.

❑ The text is redrawn using the new styles to set the text spacing in bold italic characters.

Basic steps

1　Click on the text tool or press [T].

2　Click and drag the mouse across the text to highlight it.

3　Click the button on the toolbar to launch the character window.

4　Type the target web page address into the URL box.

5　Click on the stage to deselect the text and see the dotted under-line below it.

6　Press [Ctrl+Enter] then click the text to test the link.

❑　Your web browser will attempt to connect to the URL address.

Take note

Click the window's X button to exit test mode and return to normal editor mode.

Creating hyperlinks

Text can easily be turned into a clickable hyperlink by typing the target web page address into the URL box in the character window. The editor will then display the text with a dotted underline to denote that it is a hyperlink. To test the hyperlink press [Ctrl+Enter], to enter test mode, then click on the text.

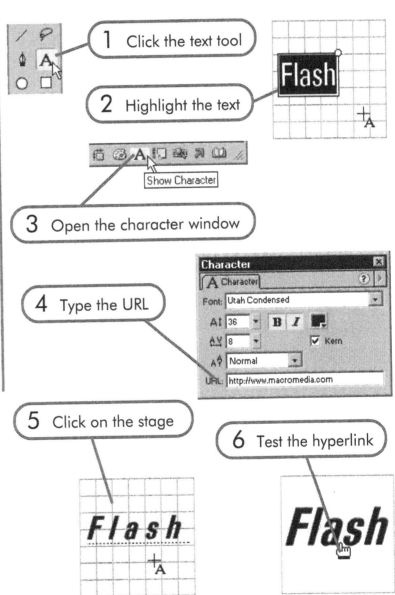

1　Click the text tool

2　Highlight the text

Show Character

3　Open the character window

4　Type the URL

5　Click on the stage

6　Test the hyperlink

Changing characters

Individual characters can be modified in an existing block of text using the character window to apply new settings. This allows some interesting effects to be created by changing the style, colour, font, spacing or size of individual characters.

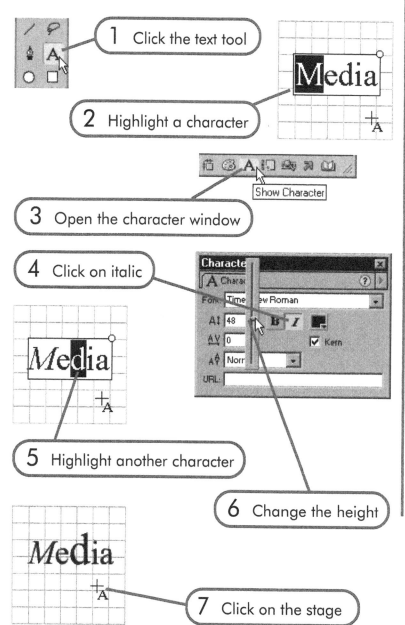

1. Click the text tool
2. Highlight a character
3. Open the character window
4. Click on italic
5. Highlight another character
6. Change the height
7. Click on the stage

1. Click on the text tool or press [T].

2. Click and drag the mouse across the text to highlight just a single character.

3. Click the button on the toolbar to launch the character window or press [Ctrl+T].

4. Click the italic button to make that character italic.

5. Click and drag the mouse across another character to modify it.

6. Click the height button and adjust the slider to make that character taller.

7. Click on the stage to deselect the text.

☐ The text now has an italic first letter and a taller middle letter.

Basic steps

1 Click on the text tool or press [T].

2 Click and drag the mouse across the text to highlight just a single character.

3 Click the button on the toolbar to launch the character window or press [Ctrl+T].

4 Click the offset button then choose the subscript menu option.

5 Click and drag the mouse across another character to modify it.

6 Click the offset button then choose the superscript menu option.

7 Click on the stage to deselect the text.

❑ The modified characters have been reduced in size and their positions have been vertically offset to the normal text.

Subscript and Superscript characters

The character window provides a means to offset characters to create raised superscript text and lowered subscript text. This is particularly useful with advisory characters such as those which signify copyright, trademark, registered name and so on.

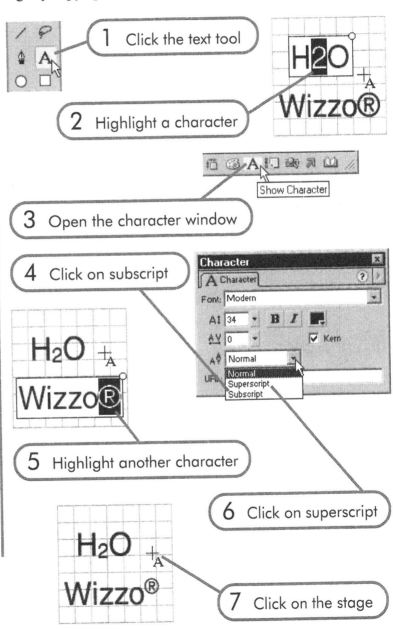

1 Click the text tool

2 Highlight a character

3 Open the character window

4 Click on subscript

5 Highlight another character

6 Click on superscript

7 Click on the stage

Text as graphics

Text can be changed into normal graphic elements which can be repositioned and modified just like any other graphic. This provides a useful start to create logo designs, or other highly stylised text, from an initial block of plain text.

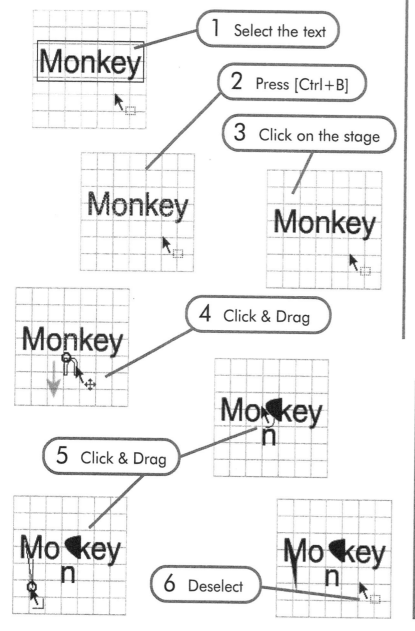

1 Select the text

2 Press [Ctrl+B]

3 Click on the stage

4 Click & Drag

5 Click & Drag

6 Deselect

Basic steps

1 Select the text to be changed to graphics.

2 Press [Ctrl+B] to break apart the text – see the text elements appear selected.

3 Click the stage to deselect the elements.

4 Click and drag an element to reposition it just like any other graphic.

5 Click and drag an element to modify it just like any other graphic.

6 Click on the stage to deselect the elements.

Take note

The text has been changed into several graphic elements and this conversion from text to graphics cannot be reversed.

Basic steps

1 Select the text to have the drop shadow.

2 Click the button in the toolbar or press [Ctrl+Alt+I] to open the info dialog box.

3 Note the coordinate position of the current text block – in this case X=95 and Y=40.

4 Press [Ctrl+D] to create a duplicate of the original text block on the stage.

5 Type new values into the X Y boxes in the info window to posi-tion the new block. Make these both less than the originals – in this case X=93,Y=38.

6 Click the fill colour block in the toolbox then choose a lighter shade for the dupli-cate text.

❑ The duplicate text now overlaps the original text to create a drop shadow effect.

Drop shadow effect

Adding a drop shadow effect is a popular way of making text stand out by creating an illusion of depth. This is easily done in Flash by duplicating the text in a lighter shade and changing the duplicate's position to be slightly offset to the original.

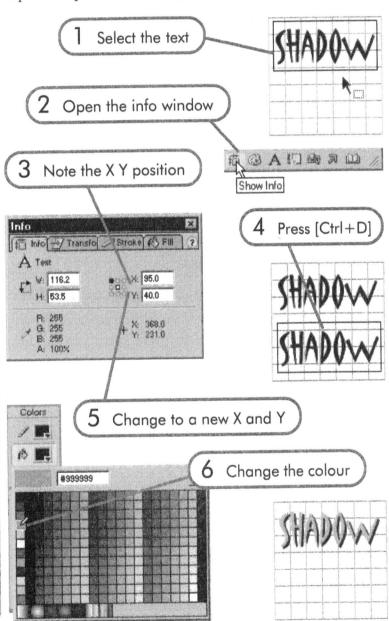

Summary

❑ The text tool is used to add text to the stage.

❑ Text appearance can be modified by changing the settings in the character window that specify colour, font and text size.

❑ Text style can also be set in the character window to specify text spacing and bold or italic text.

❑ Text can be made into a hyperlink by stating a valid target address in the character window's URL box.

❑ Flash Test mode is entered by pressing [Ctrl+Enter].

❑ Test mode can be used to test hyperlinks.

❑ Individual characters can be modified using the character window settings.

❑ Subscript and superscript text is smaller than normal text and is raised or lowered.

❑ Text can be broken apart into graphic elements that can be modified just like any other graphic element.

❑ A duplicate block of text can be used to create a drop shadow effect.

5 Thinking in layers

Creating a layer

Imagine layers as transparent sheets stacked one on top of the other. You can draw on any of these layers so that the graphics can overlap without coming into direct contact. When Flash opens an editor window the stage contains a drawing area that is designated Layer 1 by default. Additional layers can be added above this default layer to add overlapping graphics.

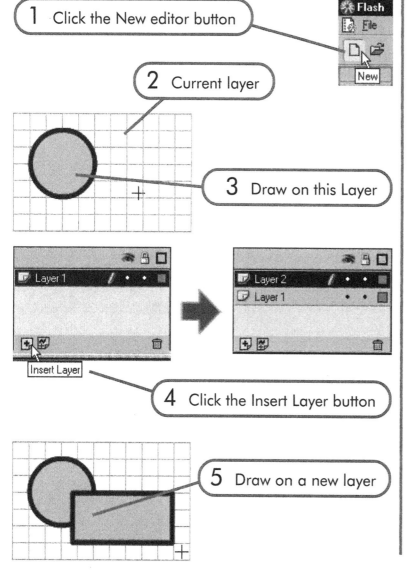

1 Click the New editor button

2 Current layer

3 Draw on this Layer

Flash
File
New

4 Click the Insert Layer button

Insert Layer

Layer 1

Layer 2
Layer 1

5 Draw on a new layer

1 Click the New button on the main toolbar or press [Ctrl+N] to open a new editor window.

Or

2 Use the existing layer in the current editor window.

3 Add an example graphic on this layer.

4 Click the Insert Layer button in the layers panel to create a new layer above the current one – see its new label added in the layers panel.

5 Add an overlapping graphic example in the new upper layer.

❑ The stage in the editor window now contains two layers with a graphic on each. The graphics overlap visually but cannot interact because they are not in direct contact with each other.

Basic steps

1 Create multiple layers in the editor with a graphic on each one.

2 Double-click on the label of a layer that is to be renamed.

3 Type a meaningful name onto the label – the new name is set when you click on the stage or another item.

4 Click all the other labels and type new names for them.

5 Click on the label of a layer to be deleted.

6 Click the trash button to delete the selected layer.

Tip

Drag a layer label over the trash icon then release the mouse button to delete that layer. Click Edit > Undo twice to recover the layer.

Controlling layers

The layers panel in the Flash editor is where all layer features are controlled. When working with a lot of layers it is advisable, and more professional, to give each layer a meaningful name. Double-click any layer's label in the layers panel then type a new name to rename that layer. To delete any layer just click its label in the layers panel then click the trash button.

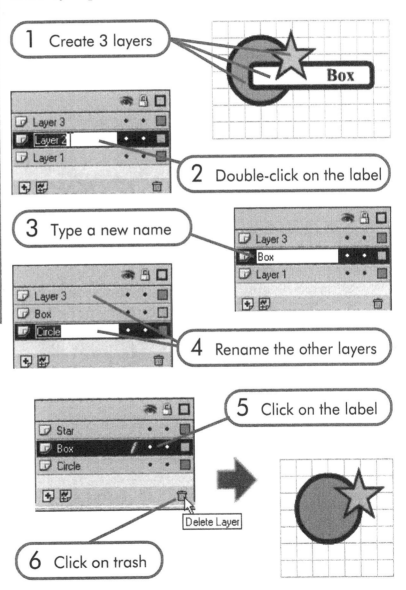

1 Create 3 layers

2 Double-click on the label

3 Type a new name

4 Rename the other layers

5 Click on the label

Delete Layer

6 Click on trash

Hiding layers

The layers panel can be used to toggle the visibility of all layers by clicking the eye icon. Individual layers can be hidden and revealed by clicking the dot on their label below the eye icon.

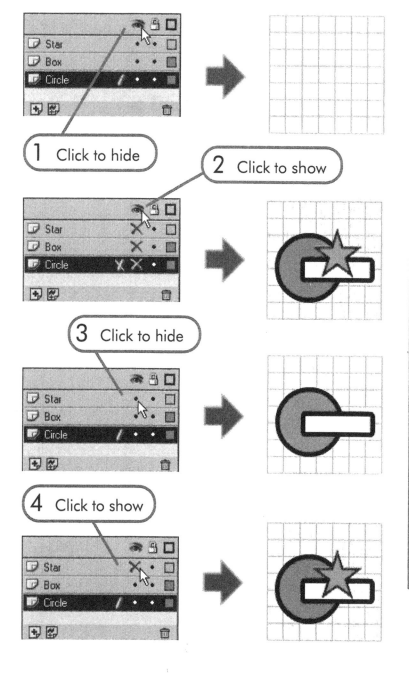

Basic steps

1 Click on the eye icon in the layers panel to hide all layers – the dots below the eye icon on each label change to crosses to signify that the layers are hidden.

2 Click the eye icon when all layers are hidden to show them once more – the crosses on each label change back to dots to signify that the layers are revealed.

3 Click the dot below the eye icon on a layer label to hide that layer – that dot changes to a cross to signify that the layer is hidden.

4 Click the cross below the eye icon on a layer label to show that layer once more – the cross changes back to a dot to signify that the layer is revealed.

Basic steps

1 Click on the lock icon in the layers panel to lock all layers – the dots on each layer label below the lock icon change to signify that each layer is safely locked.

2 Click on the outlines icon in the layers panel to show all graphics as outlines – the filled squares below the outlines icon change to empty squares to signify that each layer is only showing outlines.

3 Click on the individual outlines icon on any layer label to display full graphics again on that layer.

Or

Click on the individual lock icon on any layer label to unlock the graphics on that layer.

Handling mutiple layers

When working with several overlapping layers it is advisable to lock those layers containing finished graphics so that they cannot be accidentally altered. Click on the lock icon in the layers panel to lock all layers. To lock individual layers click on the dot below the lock icon on that layer's label.

It is sometimes helpful for clarity to view the graphics as just outlines. Click on the outlines icon in the layers panel to change all layers to outlines. To view individual layers as outlines click on the square below the outlines icon on that layer's label.

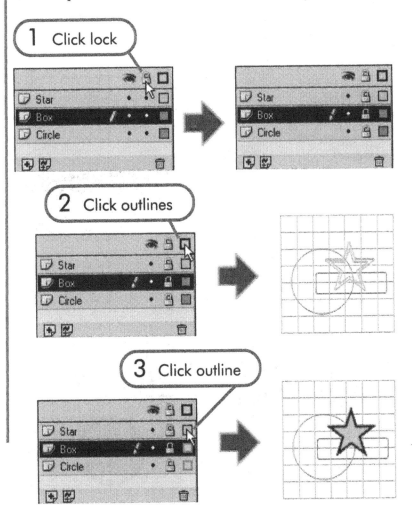

Change the stacking order

Using layers means that the position of graphics on the stage can be changed in three dimensions. As usual the position can be changed from left to right and from top to bottom by dragging the graphic with the arrow tool. Also the position can be changed from front to back by rearranging the stacking order of the layers.

The labels in the layers panel follow the current stacking order. So the label at the bottom of the panel belongs to the bottom layer on the stage with higher layers shown above. To change the stacking order just drag a label to a new position and the layers will be rearranged accordingly.

1 Click on the label of the layer to be moved.

2 Hold down the mouse and drag the label to a new position in the stacking order.

3 Release the mouse to complete the move.

❑ The stacking order of the layers is now rearranged so that graphics on higher layers will overlap those on lower layers.

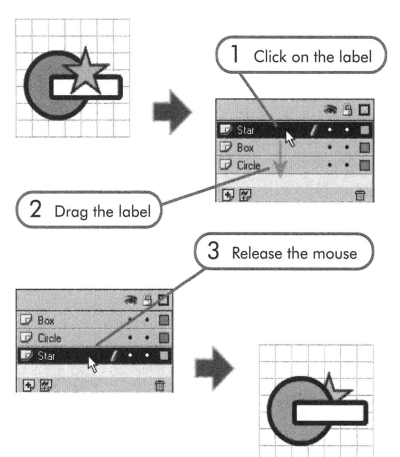

1 Click on the label

2 Drag the label

3 Release the mouse

Take note

Layered graphics are extremely useful in the creation of animations. The bottom layer can be used to display any background scenery then graphics that are to be animated can be placed on layers above.

Basic steps

1 Click on the dots under the eye icon to hide the upper layers.

2 Drag the arrow tool to select the elements to be moved.

3 Press [Ctrl+G] to group the selected elements.

4 Press [Ctrl+X] to cut the selected group onto the clipboard.

5 Click on the dots under the eye icon to show the upper layers.

6 Click on the top layer label to make it the active layer.

7 Press [Ctrl+Shift+V] to paste the selected group from the clip-board.

❑ The graphic elements that were selected and grouped on the bottom layer are now pasted onto the top layer at their original location on the stage.

Moving between layers

Graphics can be moved between layers using a cut'n'paste method to cut them from one layer then paste onto another layer. This is useful to promote a graphic to a higher level in the stacking order so changing the way that other graphics overlap.

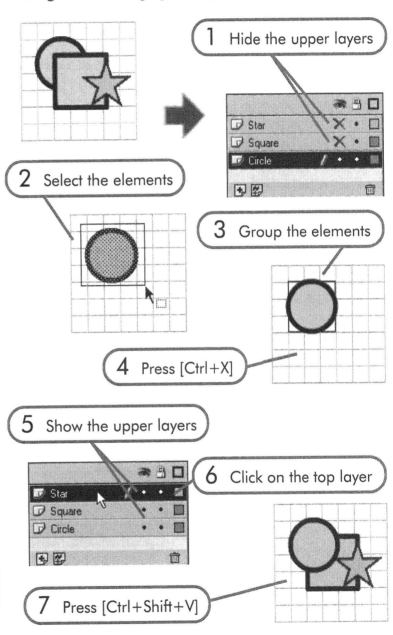

1 Hide the upper layers

2 Select the elements

3 Group the elements

4 Press [Ctrl+X]

5 Show the upper layers

6 Click on the top layer

7 Press [Ctrl+Shift+V]

Adding special layers

Guide layers hold graphic content that merely helps position items on the stage. A normal guide layer can contain lines or shapes to be used as points of reference when drawing on the stage. A layer can be made into a normal guide layer using the context menu that appears when you right-click on a layer label.

Another type of guide layer is used to guide the motion of animated objects along a path. These motion guide layers can contain just a single line that is the animation path to follow. Motion guide layers can be quickly added using the Add Guide Layer button in the Layers panel.

1   Click on the label of the layer to which you want to add a motion guide layer.

2   Click the Add Guide Layer button to add a motion guide layer to the selected layer.

3   Right-click on the label of the layer you want to make into a normal guide layer.

4   Click on the Guide item in the context menu to convert the selected layer into a normal guide layer.

❑   The motion guide layer is added to the layers panel as a separate layer label.

❑   The icon on the layer that has been converted changes to denote that it is now a normal guide layer.

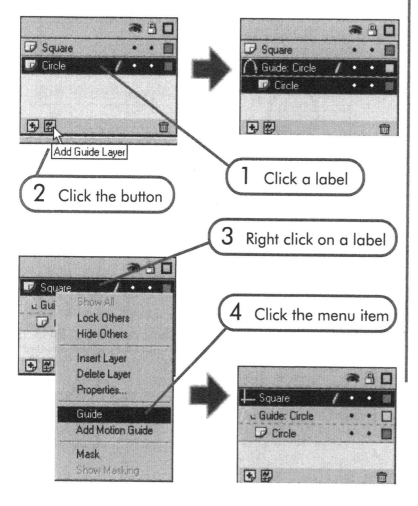

56

Basic steps

Making a mask layer

1 Click the Add Layer button to create a new layer.

2 Right click the label to open a context menu.

3 Click the Mask item on the menu to make the layer into a mask layer.

4 Click the lock icon to unlock both layers.

5 Paint any type of fill element on the mask layer as a window.

6 Finally click the lock icon again.

❑ The mask layer and the original layer are locked together – Only that part of the original layer that is covered by fill on the mask layer is visible.

A mask layer can be locked to another layer permitting only a part of that layer to be visible. Any parts of the mask layer that contain a fill element act as a window to allow the layer below to show through. To create a mask, first add a new layer then right click its label and choose Mask from the context menu.

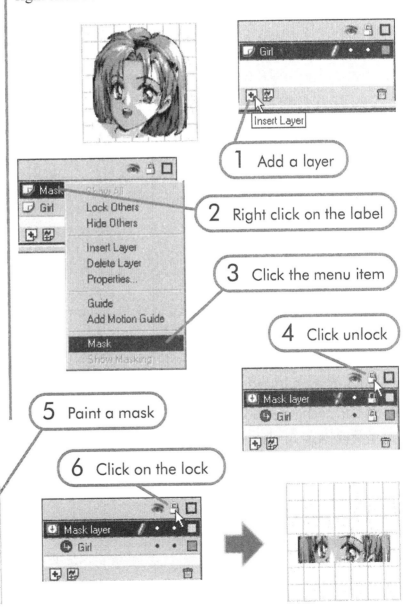

1 Add a layer

2 Right click on the label

3 Click the menu item

4 Click unlock

5 Paint a mask

6 Click on the lock

Summary

- Layers allow graphics to overlap without coming into direct contact with each other.

- Layers can be added, or deleted, in the layers panel of the editor window.

- The eye icon in the layers panel controls the visibility of each layer.

- Layers can be locked, or unlocked, with the lock icon in the layers panel.

- The graphics on each layer can be shown in outline form only, using the outline icon in the layers panel.

- Layer labels in the layers panel reflect the order in which the layers are stacked and the order can be changed by rearranging the labels.

- A layer's graphics overlap those on lower layers.

- The cut'n'paste technique is used to move graphics between layers.

- Normal guide layers are useful to aid positioning of elements on other layers.

- Motion guide layers contain a single line marking a path to be followed by an animation.

- Mask layers are used to restrict how much of the locked layer below is visible.

6 Saving graphics

The Flash library

Each Flash document is provided with a library which may be used to store components used in that movie. The library can store graphics, sounds, bitmaps, text and even entire animations such as rollover buttons (see page 114).

The advantage of storing these assets in a library is that one or more copies of any item stored in the library can be easily added to a movie. This is very useful when creating animations where the same graphic needs to be appear several times. The term 'symbol' is used to describe a graphic that has been stored in a library and each copy of the symbol is called an 'instance'.

Contents of the document library are shown in the library window that can be opened by clicking on the Show Library button in the toolbar at the bottom of the editor window.

1 Click the Show Library button on the toolbar at the bottom of the editor window, or press [Ctrl+L].

❑ The library window opens showing any symbols that have been added to the library for that document. If no symbols have been added the window will be empty.

1 Click the button

Preview

Symbol — girl — Wide view
— Narrow view

New symbol
New folder — Trash

Tip

Click the Wide view button to enlarge the library window.

Take note

Using symbol instances is a very efficient way to reuse graphics while still keeping the movie file size small.

Add a symbol to the library

1 Use the arrow tool to select the graphic to store as a Symbol.

2 Press [F8] to open the Symbol Properties dialog box.

3 Type a name for the new symbol in the Name text field.

4 Click on the radio button to create a static graphic symbol.

5 Click the OK button to create the symbol.

❑ The Symbol Properties dialog box closes and the new symbol appears in the library window.

❑ The selected graphic on the stage gains a crosshair at its centre point to denote that it is now an instance of the stored symbol.

To store a graphic from the stage in the library requires that it is first converted into a symbol. Select the graphic to be stored then press [F8] to open the Symbol Properties dialog box. Specify a name and type of symbol then press the OK button to convert the graphic to a symbol. The stored symbol will then be available from the library window.

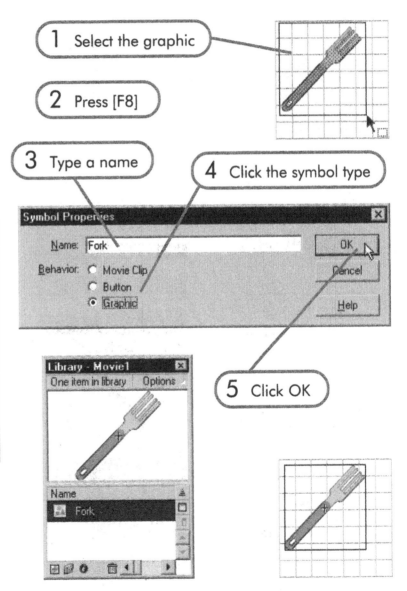

Make a library folder

Symbols in the library window can be put into folders to make it easier to work with larger numbers of them. The New Folder button creates a new folder in the library window that can be named to represent the symbols it contains. Drag a symbol icon onto the folder icon to add that symbol to the folder.

1 Click the New Folder button.

2 Type a meaningful name for the new folder.

3 Click on a symbol and drag it over the folder icon to move it.

❑ When the mouse button is released the symbol is moved into the folder. The symbol icon is depicted offset to signify the symbol is now inside a folder.

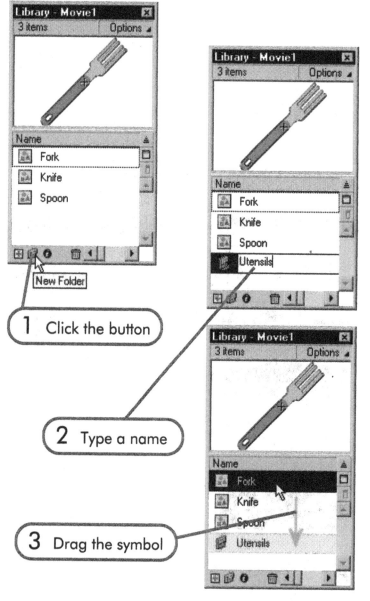

1 Click the button

2 Type a name

3 Drag the symbol

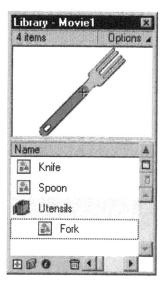

Basic steps

1 Click on a symbol in the library window to select it for deletion.

2 Click the trash icon Delete button in the library window.

3 If you are sure that this symbol and all its instances are to be deleted, click the Delete button in the Delete dialog box.

❑ The deleted symbol is removed from the library and all instances of it are removed from the stage.

Take note

Once deleted, symbols cannot be recovered.

Deleting symbols

Symbols can be deleted from the library using the Delete button depicted by the trash icon. It is important to note that when a symbol is deleted all instances of that symbol are removed from the stage. This process cannot be undone so Flash presents a warning dialog box to remind you and asks for a confirmation before making the deletion.

1 Click a symbol

2 Click the Delete button

3 Click the Delete button

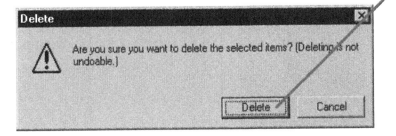

Delete

⚠ Are you sure you want to delete the selected items? (Deleting is not undoable.)

Delete   Cancel

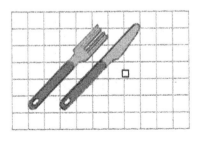

Using symbol instances

Graphics that are stored as symbols in the library can be quickly replicated on the stage. Click on the library preview window of the required graphic, or its label, and drag the mouse onto the stage. This will add an instance of that symbol on the stage and can be used repeatedly to add multiple instances of that symbol.

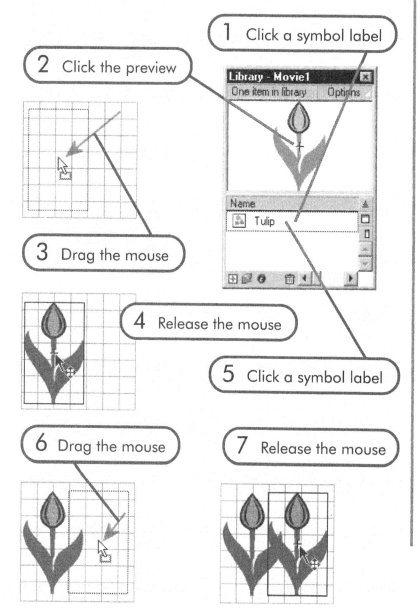

1 Click a symbol label

2 Click the preview

3 Drag the mouse

4 Release the mouse

5 Click a symbol label

6 Drag the mouse

7 Release the mouse

Library - Movie1
One item in library   Options
Name
Tulip

1 Press [Ctrl+L] to open the library then click on a symbol label – the symbol appears in the preview window.

2 Click on the symbol in the preview window.

3 Hold down the mouse button and drag the mouse onto the stage.

4 Release the mouse button to see an instance of the symbol appear on the stage.

Or

5 Click a symbol label in the library.

6 Hold down the mouse button and drag the mouse onto the stage.

7 Release the mouse button to see an instance of the symbol appear on the stage.

☐ Where instances overlap those added last will be uppermost.

Modifying instances

1 Click on the instance that is to be modified.

2 Click Window > Panels > Effect on the toolbar menu options to launch the Effect window.

3 Click the drop-down menu button to display the menu.

4 Click the menu option to chose how the instance should be modified – the Alpha option changes transparency.

5 Drag the slider to modify the transparency value of the selected instance.

❑ The overall appearance of the selected instance changes as the slider is moved.

❑ This new appearance is retained when the instance is deselected.

Instances can be scaled and rotated just like any other graphic element. Additionally their appearance can be modified to change the overall colour and transparency using the settings in the effect dialog box. This can be opened from the main Flash toolbar by clicking Window > Panels > Effect. Changing the transparency value of an instance can be used in an animated sequence to make a graphic fade-in or fade-out.

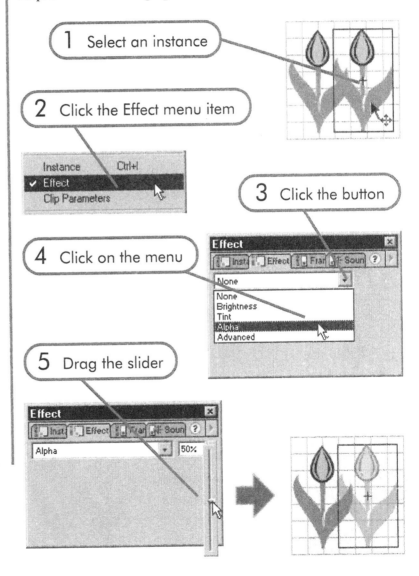

1 Select an instance

2 Click the Effect menu item

3 Click the button

4 Click on the menu

5 Drag the slider

Editing symbols

Symbol editing mode can be used to modify any symbol and the changes will instantly be made to any instances of that symbol. The Edit Symbols and Edit Scene buttons at the top right corner of the editor window can be used to enter and exit symbol editing mode. When a symbol has been chosen for editing it can be ungrouped to allow changes to be made to its elements. Choosing a scene from the Edit Scene button menu returns the editor window to normal mode showing changes that have been made.

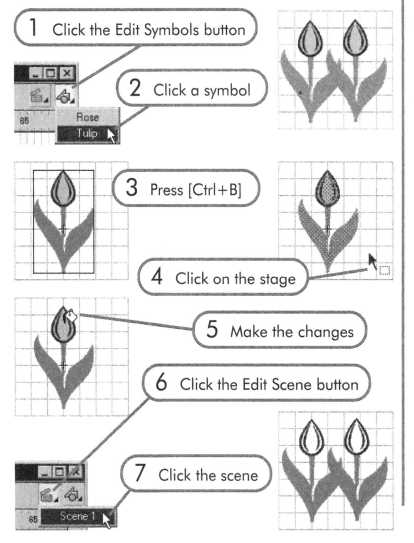

1 Click the Edit Symbols button

2 Click a symbol

3 Press [Ctrl+B]

4 Click on the stage

5 Make the changes

6 Click the Edit Scene button

7 Click the scene

1 Click on the Edit Symbols button, or press [Ctrl+E] to enter symbol editing mode.

2 Click on a symbol to be edited and this will appear in the centre of the editor window.

3 Press [Ctrl+B] to break apart the grouped symbol.

4 Click on a blank area of the stage to deselect all elements.

5 Modify the graphic elements as required – in this case change a fill colour using the paint bucket tool.

6 Click the Edit Scene button to display a menu of scenes in the current movie.

7 Click the original scene item to return to normal editing mode.

❑ The symbol and all its instances now appear in modified form.

Basic steps

1 Select an instance on the stage of a symbol that you want to duplicate.

2 Press [Ctrl+I] to launch the Instance window.

3 Click the Duplicate Symbol button in the Instance window to open the Symbol Name dialog box.

4 Accept the suggested name, or type another name into the Symbol Name text field, then press the OK button.

❏ A duplicate symbol is created and appears in the library window with the given name.

Duplicating symbols

A duplicate copy of an existing symbol can be easily made using the Duplicate Symbol button in the Instance dialog box. This second symbol could then be modified to quickly create a variation to the original symbol. The Instance window can be launched by pressing [Ctrl+I].

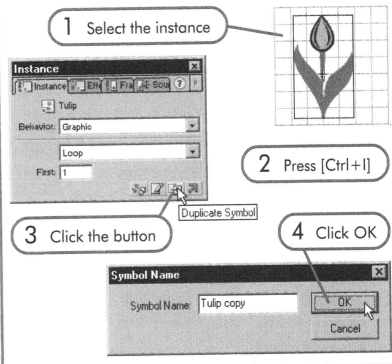

1 Select the instance

2 Press [Ctrl+I]

3 Click the button

Duplicate Symbol

4 Click OK

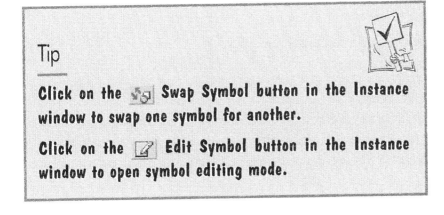

Tip

Click on the 🔁 **Swap Symbol button in the Instance window to swap one symbol for another.**

Click on the ✏️ **Edit Symbol button in the Instance window to open symbol editing mode.**

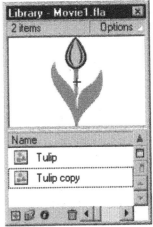

Summary

❑ Every Flash document has a library that can be used to store graphics, sounds, bitmaps, text and entire animations for that movie.

❑ A graphic stored in the library is called a symbol and copies of the symbol are called instances.

❑ [F8] opens the Symbol Properties dialog which is used to convert a graphic to a symbol.

❑ Stored symbols can be organised into folders in the library window to make them easier to find.

❑ Symbols can be deleted using the library's Delete button and once deleted they cannot be recovered.

❑ Deleting a symbol also deletes all instances of that symbol from the stage.

❑ Instances of a symbol are created on the stage by dragging from the library window.

❑ Individual instances can be scaled and rotated.

❑ The Effect window can be used to adjust the overall colour or transparency of an instance.

❑ A symbol can be edited in symbol editing mode.

❑ Editing a symbol instantly changes all instances of that symbol on the stage.

❑ Symbols can be duplicated using the Duplicate Symbol button in the Instance window.

7 Using other graphics

Importing graphics

Flash graphics are stored as a series of shapes and fills. This type of graphic is called a vector graphic. Vector graphics are more efficient than bitmaps which need to store information about every single pixel in the graphic. Also vector graphics can be scaled up or down without loss of clarity, unlike bitmaps.

Flash can use vector graphics that have been created in other popular vector graphic applications such as Macromedia Freehand and Adobe Illustrator as well as Metafile (WMF) and Enhanced Metafile (EMF) formats. To select a vector file to import into a Flash movie, click Import on the toolbar's File menu or press the [Ctrl+R].

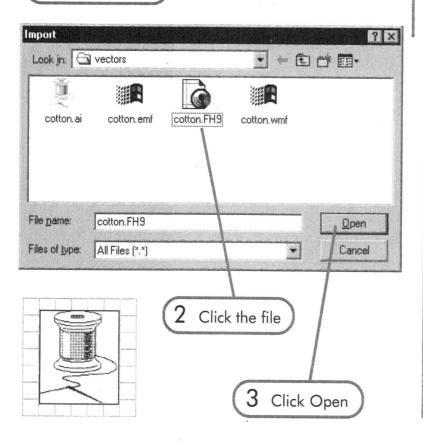

1 Press [Ctrl+R]

2 Click the file

3 Click Open

Basic steps

1 Click File > Import on the main Flash toolbar, or press [Ctrl+R], to open the Import dialog box.

2 Navigate to the file to be imported and click on it to select it.

3 Click Open in the Import dialog box.

❑ The chosen vector graphic is added at the centre of the stage and on a new layer.

Take note

Macromedia provides special support for importing Freehand files. An additional Freehand Import dialog box opens to allow further control of how the graphic will appear on the Stage.

70

Basic steps

1. Click File > Import on the main Flash toolbar, or press [Ctrl+R], to open the Import dialog box.

2. Navigate to the file to be imported and click on it to select it.

3. Click Open in the Import dialog box.

❑ The chosen bitmap graphic is added at the centre of the stage on the current layer and its symbol is added to the Library.

Take note

An special additional Import dialog box opens to provide extra settings when importing bitmaps in the PNG file format that is favoured by Macromedia's Fireworks application.

Importing bitmaps

Flash can import bitmap graphics in the popular file formats of GIF, JPG, BMP and PNG. This allows you to use your favourite graphics application to create a non-vector graphic for use in Flash. If imported GIF or PNG graphics include any transparent areas, Flash will preserve that transparency in the graphic that is placed on the stage. To select a bitmap file to import into a Flash movie click File > Import on the toolbar or press **[Ctrl+R]**.

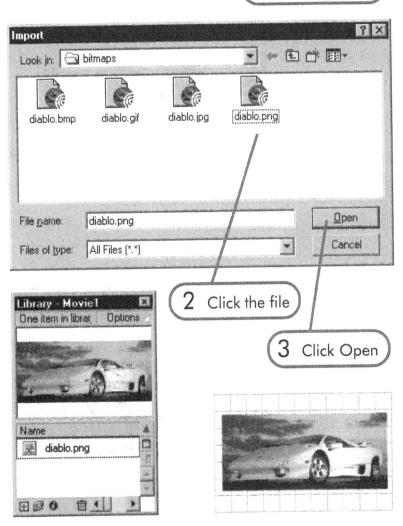

1 Press [Ctrl+R]

2 Click the file

3 Click Open

Converting bitmaps

Imported graphics can be converted into vector graphics so they can be modified in Flash. With an imported bitmap selected on the stage, click Modify > Trace Bitmap on the Flash toolbar to open the Trace Bitmap dialog box. When you press the OK button in this dialog box the bitmap is converted into vector elements that can be modified like any other element. The former background area can then be deleted to leave the main graphic.

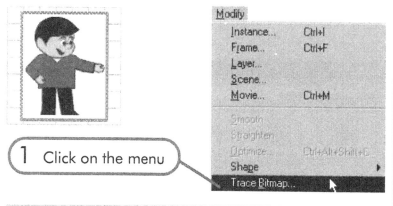

1 Click on the menu

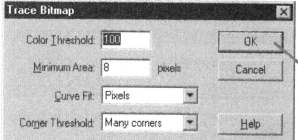

2 Click OK

1 With the bitmap selected on the stage, click Modify >Trace Bitmap on the main Flash toolbar.

2 Click OK to accept the default trace settings.

3 Click a blank area of the stage to deselect all selected elements.

4 Click on the background elements to select them.

5 Press [Delete] to delete those elements.

❏ The graphic is now a vector with the former background removed.

3 Click on the stage

4 Click the element

5 Press [Delete]

Basic steps

1. Change the default setting of 100 to specify if Flash should be more, or less, discerning when grouping colours.

2. Change the default setting from 8 to specify how many pixels to include in the colour calculation.

3. Click the button to open the drop down menu then choose how tightly Flash should draw outlines.

4. Click the button to open the drop down menu then choose how sharply Flash should draw corners.

☐ When the OK button is pressed in the Trace Bitmap dialog box, Flash creates vector shapes resembling the original bitmap using the specified settings.

Trace Bitmap dialog settings

The result of converting a bitmap to a vector graphic is not an exact duplication of the original graphic but an approximation of it with a set of vector shapes. Four settings in the Trace Bitmap dialog box control how accurately these shapes trace the colour areas in the original bitmap graphic.

● Color Threshold is a range of 1 to 500 that specifies how similar adjacent colours will be grouped together. Higher settings make Flash less discerning and produce fewer final vector shapes, so reducing the file size.

● Minimum Area is a range of 1 to 1,000 that specifies how many pixels Flash should use when calculating the colour.

● Curve Fit specifies how accurately Flash should draw the outline around the final vector shapes.

● Corner Threshold specifies if Flash should draw sharp corners or more rounded corners.

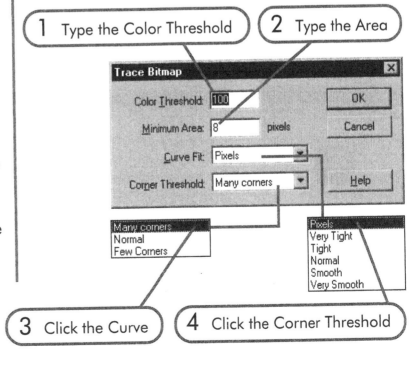

1 Type the Color Threshold 2 Type the Area

3 Click the Curve 4 Click the Corner Threshold

Importing animations

Flash can import animated GIFs into the movie in much the same way as importing a single graphic in the GIF file format. Flash recreates the individual frame images in the original animation and places them in the timeline panel as separate frames on the current layer. Each of the frames are also added to the library as separate bitmap symbols.

1 Press [Ctrl+R]

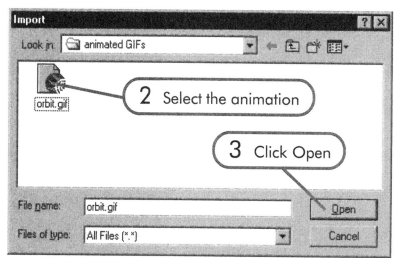

2 Select the animation

3 Click Open

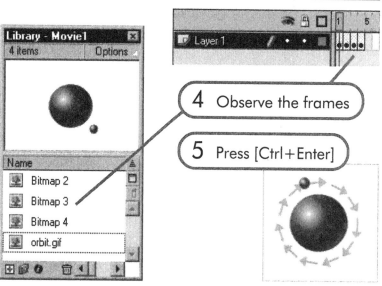

4 Observe the frames

5 Press [Ctrl+Enter]

1 Press [Ctrl+R] or click File > Import on the Flash toolbar to open the Import dialog box.

2 Click on the animated GIF file to select it.

3 Click Open to import the animation file graphics into Flash – the graphic of the first frame in the animation sequence appears on the stage.

4 Notice that the animation graphics appear as individual bitmap symbols in the library and also as individual frames on the current layer in the timeline.

5 Press [Ctrl+Enter] to test the movie and run the animation.

❏ You will learn how to create animations in Flash in the next chapter of this book.

Basic steps

1 Click on the first file in the series to select it.

2 Click Open to import the graphic and see a dialog box appear asking if you want to import the entire sequence.

3 Click Yes to import the sequence – the first graphic appears on the stage.

4 See the individual bitmap symbols appear in the library and individual frames appear in the timeline.

❑ The sequence can be run as an animation.

Importing a sequence of graphics

Flash has an intelligent option to import a sequence of graphics to be used as an animation. If the files are within a single folder and have the same name with a different ending number, Flash recognises the sequence and offers to import them all together.

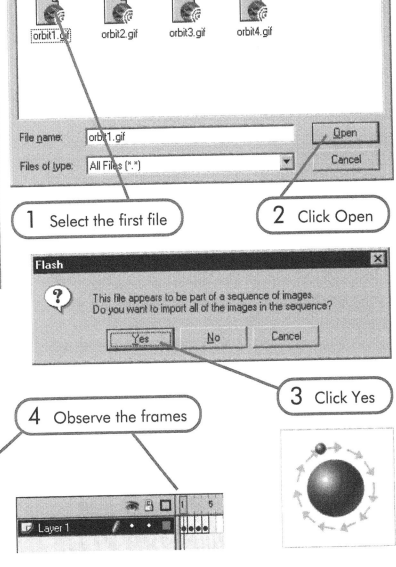

1 Select the first file

2 Click Open

3 Click Yes

4 Observe the frames

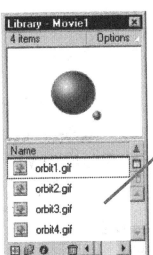

Bitmaps as fills

Flash allows an imported bitmap to be used as a fill pattern in place of a solid fill colour. This creates a repeating tiled pattern of the bitmap in the filled area and can be applied with any of the tools that create a fill – oval, rectangle, paintbrush and paint bucket tools.

The bitmap first needs to be broken apart, using [Ctrl+B], then selected with the eyedropper tool. Once selected, the bitmap appears in the fill colour block in the toolbox Colors panel and can be painted onto the stage.

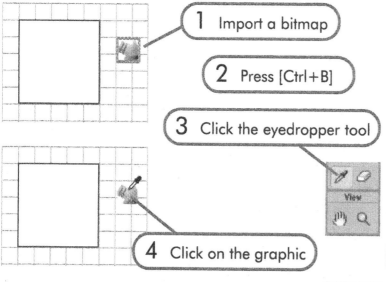

1 Import a bitmap

2 Press [Ctrl+B]

3 Click the eyedropper tool

4 Click on the graphic

5 Click the paint bucket

6 Paint the fill

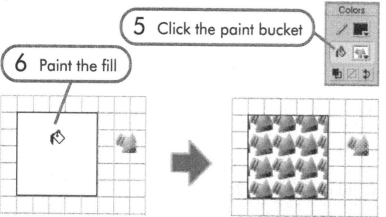

1 Import a bitmap to be used as a fill pattern.

2 Press [Ctrl+B] to break apart the imported graphic.

3 Click the eyedropper icon in the toolbox to select it.

4 Click on the imported graphic on the Stage to select the pattern.

5 Click the paint bucket icon in the toolbox to select it. Notice that the fill colour block displays the graphic pattern.

6 Click on a fill element to paint it with the fill pattern.

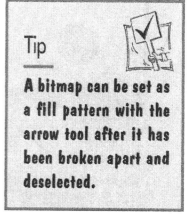

Tip

A bitmap can be set as a fill pattern with the arrow tool after it has been broken apart and deselected.

Basic steps

1 With the paint bucket tool selected, click on the Transform Fill button in the toolbox options panel.

2 Click on a bitmap fill on the stage and see the handles appear.

3 Click and drag a round handle to rotate all the tiles in the fill.

4 Click and drag a square handle to scale or skew all the tiles in the bitmap fill.

❑ The whole fill adopts these modifications.

Take note

The Lock Fill modifier can be used to prevent accidental fill changes. Make sure that the Lock Fill button is NOT selected before trying to use the Transform Fill modifier.

Modifying bitmap fills

Bitmap fills can be repositioned, scaled, rotated and skewed using the Transform Fill modifier that is available in the toolbox options panel whenever the paint bucket tool is selected. With the Transform Fill modifier selected, just click on a bitmap fill on the stage to produce a set of handles that can be dragged to manipulate the tiles within that fill. The centre handle can be used to drag the tile to a new location and the outer handles used to change the tile shape. All other tiles within the fill will repeat these modifications throughout the pattern.

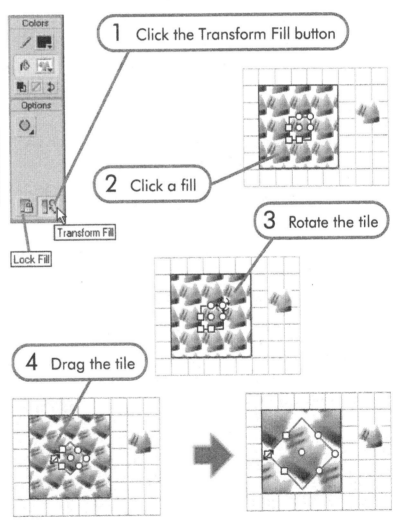

1 Click the Transform Fill button

2 Click a fill

3 Rotate the tile

4 Drag the tile

Summary

❑ Images that are created on the Flash stage are saved as vector graphics.

❑ Saving graphics as vectors is far more efficient that saving them as bitmaps.

❑ Vector graphics that have been created using Adobe Illustrator or Macromedia Freehand can be easily imported into Flash.

❑ Bitmap graphics in GIF, JPG, BMP and PNG formats can also be imported into Flash.

❑ Imported bitmaps can be converted to vector graphics using the Trace Bitmap dialog box.

❑ The Trace Bitmap settings can specify precisely how the vector shapes should be created.

❑ Complete animations in the GIF file format can be imported into Flash.

❑ A numbered sequence of bitmap graphics can be imported into Flash to create an animation.

❑ Each animation frame is shown in the timeline.

❑ [Ctrl+Enter] is used to test a Flash movie and will run an animated sequence of frames.

❑ A bitmap can be selected as a fill pattern.

❑ Bitmap fills can be modified using the Transform Fill modifier that is an available option when the paint bucket tool is selected.

8 Animating graphics

The Flash timeline

Animation requires a number of images, that are each slightly different to one another, to be displayed in sequence. If they are shown fast enough the eye cannot tell that they are individual images, so the illusion of smooth motion is created. Each one of the images is called a 'frame'.

Typical animations can have lots of frames but these can be broken down into 'keyframes', which define a new movement, and 'in-between' frames, that just display incremental changes between one keyframe and the next. Animation studios would historically employ their best artists to create keyframes then use lower-paid ones to laboriously produce the in-between frames.

Flash uses the same process to create animations but can automatically create the in-between frames for you. Each frame is shown in the Flash timeline panel with keyframes denoted by a bullet point. When a Flash movie is played each of the frames in the timeline will be displayed in succession at a specified rate. A red line indicates the current frame. To select a different frame just click on it in the timeline panel.

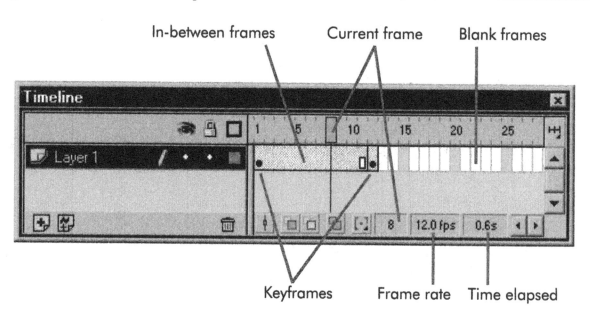

In-between frames   Current frame   Blank frames

Keyframes   Frame rate   Time elapsed

80

Basic steps

1 Click on the grey area at the top of the timeline panel then drag the mouse to detach the timeline from the window.

2 Click the button at the top right corner of the timeline to open the frame view menu.

3 Click on the Large option in the frame view menu.

4 Click on the Preview option in the frame view menu.

❑ The timeline frame segments are larger and show a preview of each keyframe.

Tip

Use the Preview In Context option to show a thumbnail preview of the entire stage in each keyframe segment.

Timeline frame views

The timeline panel can be detached from the editor window and the appearance of its frame scale can be customised using a special frame view menu. This menu is opened by clicking the button at the top right corner of the timeline panel. Options allow the size of each frame segment to be increased and include a preview of the actual content of each keyframe. This is very useful to identify the content of each keyframe at a glance.

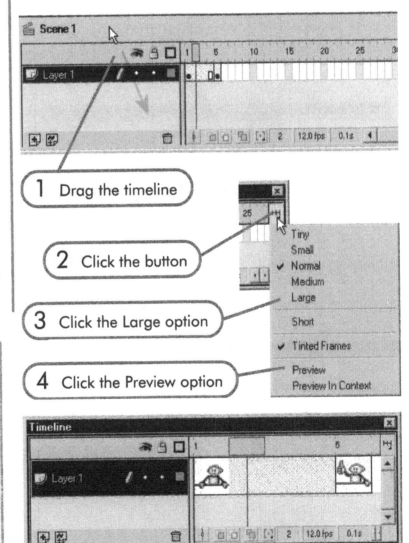

1 Drag the timeline

2 Click the button

3 Click the Large option

4 Click the Preview option

Creating keyframes

A blank keyframe can be added to the timeline to provide a blank stage where a new image can be created in an animated sequence. All the frames between the new blank keyframe and the first keyframe automatically gain the image content of that first keyframe. The new keyframe is initially blank but will contain the new image that is created on the stage to form a new frame in the animation sequence.

To insert a new blank keyframe first select a frame on the timeline then press [F7]. Alternatively press the right-hand mouse button and choose the Insert Blank Keyframe option from the context menu.

1 Click on an empty frame in the timeline.

2 Right-click on the timeline to open a context menu.

3 Click the Insert Blank keyframe option.

Or

4 Click on an empty frame in the timeline then press [F7].

❑ The chosen frame gains an outline to mark it as a blank keyframe.

❑ All frames between the new blank keyframe and the first keyframe become grey to denote that they are now in-between frames.

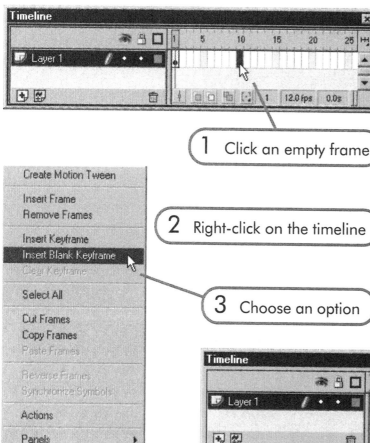

1 Click an empty frame

2 Right-click on the timeline

3 Choose an option

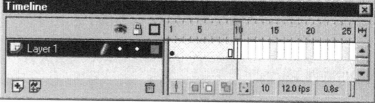

Basic steps

1 Click on an empty frame in the timeline.

2 Right-click then choose the Insert Keyframe option from the context menu – or just press [F6].

3 Modify the graphic on the stage to create the next frame in the animation sequence.

4 Press [Ctrl+Enter] to test the movie.

❑ The modified graphic is displayed on the timeline in the new keyframe.

❑ The movie displays the frames in succession to animate the frame graphics.

Take note

A new Flash document has by default one layer and one blank keyframe.

Duplicating keyframes

It is often useful to duplicate the previous keyframe content in a new keyframe so that the graphic can be modified slightly to continue an animation sequence. To duplicate a keyframe use the Insert Keyframe option in the context menu or [F6].

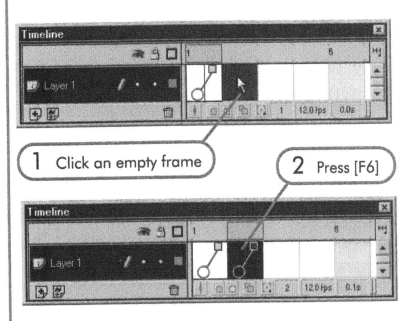

1 Click an empty frame

2 Press [F6]

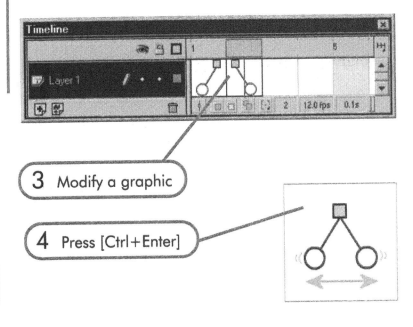

3 Modify a graphic

4 Press [Ctrl+Enter]

Handling frames

The frames that appear between keyframes have a special relationship with the first keyframe because they each display its content. Additionally they provide an area in which to create intermediate tweened animation between the first keyframe and the next, as detailed in the next chapter. These in-between frames can be added to the timeline with [F5] or by choosing the Insert Frame option from the timeline's context menu.

Basic steps

1 On a timeline with two keyframes click the first keyframe.

2 Press [F5].

Or

3 Right-click to open the context menu then choose the Insert Frame option.

4 Repeat using either [F5] or the context menu to add further frames.

❑ New in-between frames are added to the timeline after the selected keyframe.

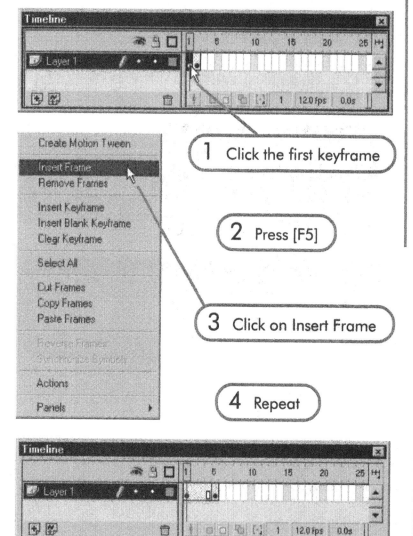

1 Click the first keyframe

2 Press [F5]

3 Click on Insert Frame

4 Repeat

Take note

The final added frame is shown with a square bullet point to denote that it is the last frame in a whole range of in-between frames.

Basic steps

1 To select a single in-between frame first position the cursor over a keyframe unit.

2 Press [Ctrl] and keep it down – see the cursor change from a hand to a pointer.

3 Click to select the required frame.

❏ The single in-between frame is now selected.

Selecting frames

The method of selecting frames in the timeline will vary depending on the type of frame and whether you want to select just a single frame or multiple frames:

● To select a single empty frame, or a single keyframe, or a single final in-between frame, just click on it.

● To select two empty frames and all the frames between them hold down [Shift] then click on the two frames.

● To select a range of empty frames hold down [Alt] while dragging across the frames.

In-between frames and their associated preceding keyframe are treated as a single unit that can be selected by clicking on any of the in-between frames. To select an individual in-between frame hold down [Ctrl] then click on it.

Tip

The appearance of the cursor in the timeline indicates the type of selection that can be made:

An entire keyframe unit can be selected with the hand cursor.

Individual frames can be selected when the cursor appears as a pointer.

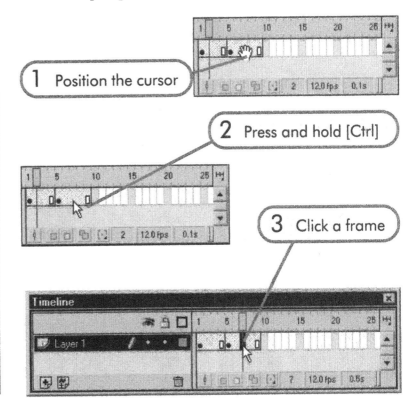

1 Position the cursor

2 Press and hold [Ctrl]

3 Click a frame

Cut'n'paste frames

A frame can be cut, or copied, from its position in the timeline then pasted into a new position using options in the timeline's context menu. Multiple frames can also be moved in this way by initially selecting a range of frames. Because Flash immediately replaces the contents of the current frame it is a good idea to always paste frames into empty frames or in-between frames. This prevents accidentally replacing the contents of a keyframe. Unwanted keyframes can be deleted separately when you are sure they are no longer required.

If a keyframe is cut from the timeline, the next in-between frame will automatically become a keyframe with the same content as the cut keyframe.

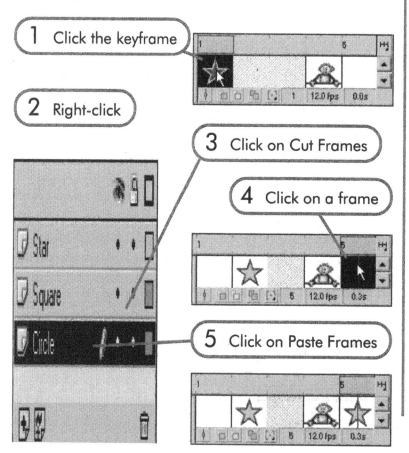

1 Click on the keyframe that you want to cut.

2 Right-click on the timeline to open the context menu.

3 Click on the Cut Frames menu option to cut the selected keyframe onto the clipboard.

❑ The preview graphic disappears from the selected keyframe and the next in-between frame becomes a new keyframe with the same content.

4 Click on the empty frame or in-between frame where you want to paste the graphic.

5 Right-click to reopen the context menu then select the Paste Frames menu option.

❑ The contents of the clipboard are pasted into the selected frame as a new keyframe.

Drag'n'drop frames

1 Click on a frame or keyframe unit that you want to copy or move and hold down the mouse.

2 Press and hold down [Alt] if you want to copy the selection – do not press [Alt] if you want to move the selection.

3 Drag the selection to the required location on the timeline.

4 Release the button/s to place the selection at the new location.

Flash allows frames to be dragged around the timeline to reposition a single frame or multiple frames. Also copies of an existing frame, or frames, can be dragged to a new location. This is a faster method than using the context menu options. To drag a keyframe unit to a new location first click on one of its in-between frames and hold down the mouse button. Move the cursor along the timeline to the new required location. The cursor hand changes to a clenched hand when dragging frames and a preview box shows where the frames will be positioned. When the mouse button is released the move is completed.

To drag a copy of an original keyframe, or keyframe unit, hold down [Alt] while dragging the cursor to the new location.

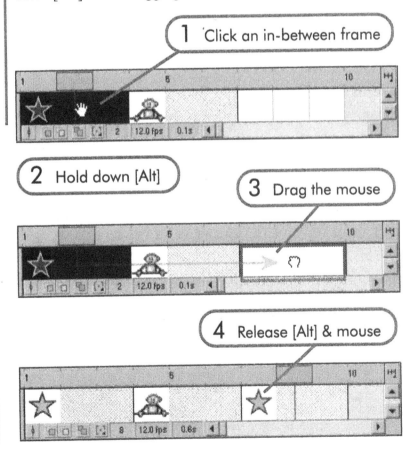

1 Click an in-between frame

2 Hold down [Alt]

3 Drag the mouse

4 Release [Alt] & mouse

Take note

The original frames remain intact if the [Alt] key is used to drag a copy of these frames. The original frames will become empty frames if the Alt key is not used.

Deleting frames

The timeline context menu has two menu options that can be used to remove content from the animation sequence. It is important to clearly understand the difference between these two options to avoid deleting content unintentionally. The Clear Keyframe option removes the graphic content from a keyframe and changes its status to make it into a regular in-between frame. The Remove Frames option removes the frame, and also its content if it is a keyframe, from the timeline completely.

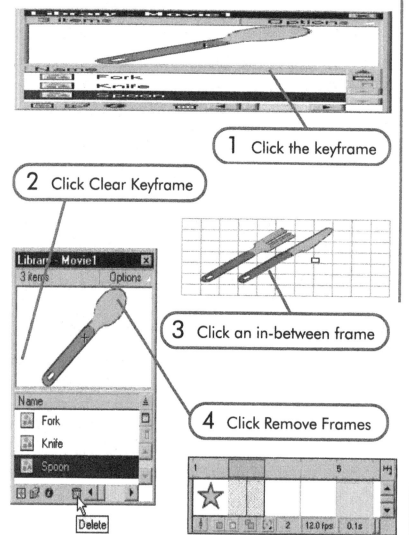

1 Click the keyframe

2 Click Clear Keyframe

3 Click an in-between frame

4 Click Remove Frames

1 Click on a keyframe that you want to clear.

2 Right-click to open the context menu then choose the Clear Keyframe option.

❑ Keyframe content is removed and the frame becomes an in-between frame.

3 Click on the in-between frame that you want to remove.

4 Right-click to reopen the context menu and choose the Remove Frames option – or press [Delete].

❑ The frame is deleted from the timeline.

Take note

Only the Remove Frames option will reduce the total number of frames in the movie.

Animation preview

1 Click on the playhead and drag it back or forwards to preview the frames animating.

Or

2 Click the Window > Toolbars > Controller options to open the Controller dialog box.

3 Click the Play button to animate the frames in the editor window.

When you test a movie, using [Ctrl+Enter], Flash first saves the movie as a file with a .swf extension then plays that file in a test window. There are other ways to quickly preview the animation directly in the Flash editor without creating a swf file. The simplest preview method is to manually drag the playhead back and forth in the area at the top of the timeline. Alternatively Flash provides a Controller dialog box with VCR-style buttons that can be used to play the animation. The Controller dialog box is opened by selecting Window > Toolbars > Controller on the main Flash toolbar.

Tip

Unless the playback is set to loop, the Play button will display the current frame up to the final frame only once. To set the playback to always loop select the Loop Playback option on the toolbar Control menu. The animation will then play repeatedly until you press the Stop button.

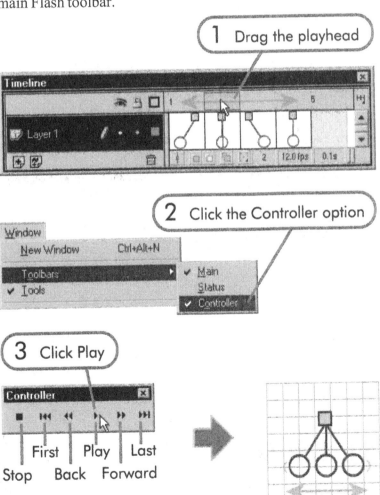

1 Drag the playhead

2 Click the Controller option

3 Click Play

Stop First Play Last
      Back Forward

Onion skinning

Flash provides a great feature that makes it easy to align frame content with that of surrounding frames by showing their content in dimmed form on the current stage. This is called the Onion Skin mode and is turned on by a button at the bottom of the timeline panel. There is also an Onion Skin Outlines mode button that allows the surrounding frame content to be shown only as outlines on the current stage. When either Onion Skin mode is selected, Onion Markers appear in the timeline over frames included in the Onion Skin view. The range of included frames can be adjusted using the Modify Onion Markers menu that is available from another button in the timeline panel. Choose the Onion 2 option to display 2 frames each side of the current frame. The Onion 5 option increases the range to 5 on each side and Onion All displays all the frames.

Basic steps

1 Click the button to open the Modify Onion Markers menu.

2 Click the Onion 2 option to include 2 frames on each side of the current frame in the Onion Skin view.

3 Click the Onion Skin button to turn on Onion Skin mode.

❑ Surrounding frames are now shown dimmed on the stage.

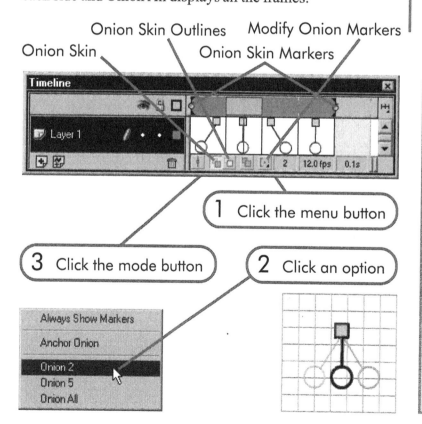

Onion Skin Outlines   Modify Onion Markers
Onion Skin   Onion Skin Markers

1 Click the menu button

3 Click the mode button   2 Click an option

Always Show Markers
Anchor Onion
Onion 2
Onion 5
Onion All

Tip

To specify a custom range of frames to be included in the Onion Skin view drag the Onion Skin Markers in the timeline to your desired frames then click the Anchor Onion option in the Modify Onion Markers menu.

Basic steps

1 Click the button to open the Modify Onion Markers menu.

2 Select the Onion All option on the menu to include all frames.

3 Click the Edit Multiple Frames button to show all frame elements.

4 Select the elements to be repositioned.

5 Drag the selection to their new position.

❑ The elements are simultaneously reposi- tioned in each frame.

Multi-frame editing

To change the position of an animated element requires its position to be changed in every frame. To modify each frame individually is tedious and can lead to errors. Edit Multiple Frames mode overcomes this by allowing you to change the position of an element in multiple frames simultaneously.

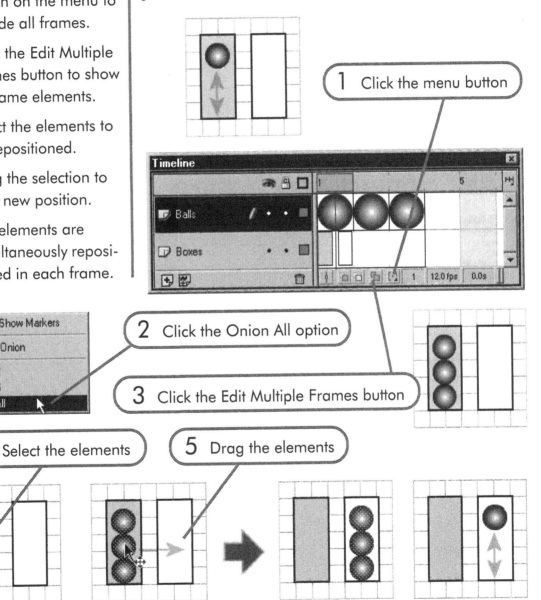

1 Click the menu button

2 Click the Onion All option

3 Click the Edit Multiple Frames button

4 Select the elements

5 Drag the elements

Always Show Markers
Anchor Onion
Onion 2
Onion 5
Onion All

Frame rate

Frame rate is the speed at which movies display successive frames. This speed is expressed as the number of frames per second (fps) that are displayed. The frame rate needs to be fast enough to create the illusion of animation but not so fast that the images become blurred. A frame rate that is too slow must also be avoided as it would allow the viewer to discern the individual frame images.

The standard frame rate for movie film is 24 frames per second. Internet animations however are best displayed at 12 frames per second so this is used as the default frame rate by Flash. A custom frame rate can be specified for an entire Flash movie by changing the default rate in the Movie Properties dialog box.

1 Double-click the frame rate box at the bottom of the timeline, or press [Ctrl+M], to open the Movie Properties dialog box.

2 Enter a new value in the frame rate field to specify the number of frames per second to be displayed.

3 Click [OK] to apply the new frame rate to the movie.

❑ The movie will display at the specified rate whenever it is played.

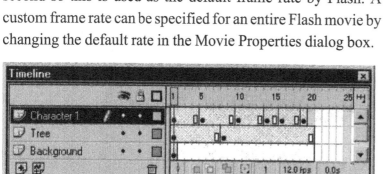

Current frame

Frame rate — Seconds

2 Type a number

1 Double-click on fps

Take note

Only one single frame rate can be specified for an entire movie.

Movie Properties

Frame Rate: `12` fps

Dimensions: Width `550 px` × Height `400 px`

Match: Printer   Contents

Background Color:

Ruler Units: `Pixels`

OK

Cancel

Save Default

Help

3 Click OK

Basic steps

1 Click the frame where you want to slow down the animation.

2 Press [F5] twice to add two following in-between frames.

3 Press [F6] twice to insert keyframes into both of the new in-between frames.

4 Click on each new keyframe in turn and modify the position of the graphic element on the stage.

❑ The animation is now slowed at the start. In this example the ball slowly climbs an incline before dropping down the far side.

Tip

To precisely position a selected object use the directional arrow keys on the keyboard.

Varying animation speeds

Although the frame rate cannot be adjusted for individual parts of a movie the animation speed can be speeded up, or slowed down, by changing the number of frames in a sequence. Adding frames will slow the animation by taking longer to complete a particular movement. Extra frames could be simple in-between frames but the animation will be smoother if the added frames are keyframes showing the graphic at intermediate positions.

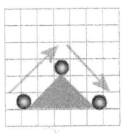

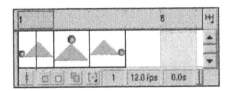
1 Click a frame

2 Press [F5] twice

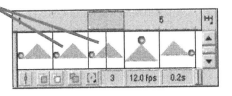
3 Press [F6] twice

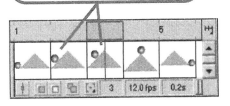
4 Modify each graphic

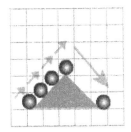

Summary

❏ The illusion of movement is created by displaying a sequence of images in rapid succession.

❏ Each image in an animated sequence is called a frame.

❏ The timeline controls the frames in a Flash movie.

❏ Frames which contain new content are called keyframes.

❏ In-between frames contain incremental changes between keyframes and can be generated by Flash.

❏ The Frame View menu can be used to alter the appearance of the frames on the timeline.

❏ [F5] can add in-between frames.

❏ [F6] can insert keyframes.

❏ You can cut'n'paste or drag'n'drop frames to relocate them on the timeline.

❏ [Delete] can be used to delete frames.

❏ The Controller window provides VCR-style buttons with which to preview a Flash movie.

❏ Onion Skin view shows a dimmed version of graphics from surrounding frames on the stage to make alignment of frame graphics easier.

❏ Elements in several frames can be simultaneously repositioned in Edit Multiple Frames mode.

❏ The Frame Rate is the speed at which the frames are displayed and can be adjusted in the Movie Properties dialog box.

9 Tweening animations

Motion tweening

The creation of intermediate frames in an animation can be automated in Flash using a process called tweening. This is a powerful feature of Flash where in-between frames are generated to automatically fill the animation between two keyframes. Where the position of a symbol changes in the two specified keyframes Flash will generate a series of incremental steps between the start and end positions. These intermediate frames for motion tweening effects are created using the Create Motion Tween option on the timeline's context menu.

1 Click on the frame in the timeline where you want to start the motion tween.

2 Right-click on the timeline to open its context menu.

3 Click on the Create Motion Tween option in the context menu.

❑ Flash creates the graphic as a symbol and gives it a default name in the library.

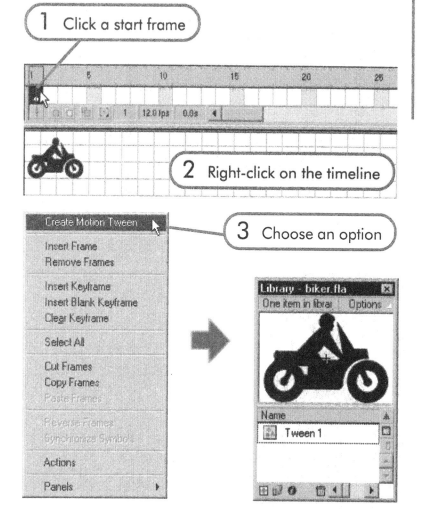

1 Click a start frame

2 Right-click on the timeline

3 Choose an option

Take note

The tweened frames are not actually new graphic frames but rather are mathematically created by Flash. This is far more efficient than making a movie with lots of keyframes and reduces the file size of the finished movie.

4 Click on the frame in the timeline where you want to end the motion tween.

5 Press [F5] to insert a frame at this selected point.

❏ A dotted line appears to indicate an incomplete motion tween.

6 With the end frame still selected click the symbol on the stage.

7 Drag the symbol to its end position – then release the mouse.

❏ The final frame is made into a keyframe.

❏ The dotted line changes to an arrow to indicate a complete motion tween.

❏ Onion Skin Outlines view can be used to show the tweening.

❏ The new motion tween animation can be previewed by pressing [Enter].

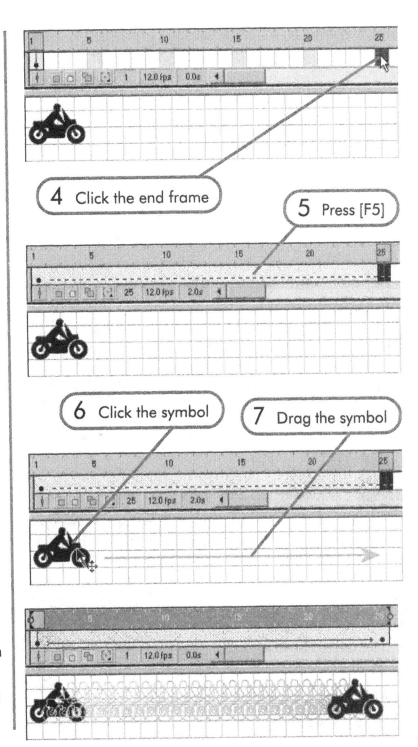

4 Click the end frame

5 Press [F5]

6 Click the symbol

7 Drag the symbol

The tweening property

An alternative way to create motion tweening is to set the tweening property of in-between frames in the Frame dialog box. This is opened by pressing [Ctrl+F] and contains a drop-down menu of the possible tweening options. Choosing the Motion option from this menu will convert the frames between two keyframes into tween frames.

1 Click on the frame in the timeline where you want to start the tweening – ensure that it contains a group or a symbol to animate.

2 Click on the frame in the timeline where you want the motion tweening to finish.

3 Press [F6] to insert a keyframe at this selected point.

1 Click a start frame

2 Click the end frame

3 Press [F6]

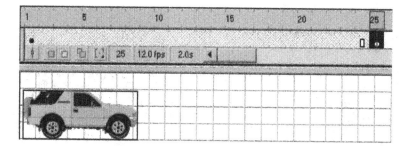

Take note

Each motion tween must have a start keyframe containing a symbol or a group, a number of in-between frames that can be converted to tween frames, and an end keyframe where the original symbol or group is repositioned.

4 With the end frame still selected, click the graphic on the stage and drag it to its end position – then release the mouse button.

5 Click on any one of the in-between frames or the first keyframe.

6 Press [Ctrl+F] to open the Frame dialog box.

7 Click the button to display the tweening property options.

8 Click on the Motion option to create the motion tween.

❑ The tweening property for all frames in the selected keyframe group is set to Motion.

❑ An arrow appears on the timeline to indicate a motion tween.

❑ The new motion tween animation can be previewed by pressing [Enter].

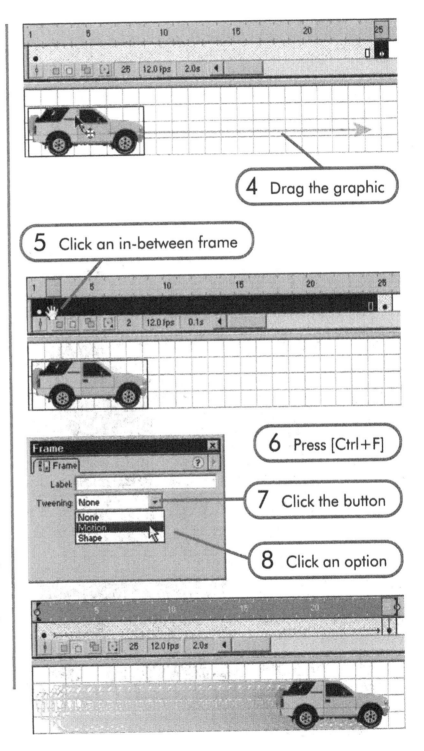

4 Drag the graphic

5 Click an in-between frame

6 Press [Ctrl+F]

7 Click the button

8 Click an option

Graphic tweening

The Motion Tween feature can be used to animate graphics in ways other than just changing their position on the stage. Tweening can automatically generate intermediate frames for changes to the size of a graphic. This can be used to grow or shrink a graphic in a Flash movie.

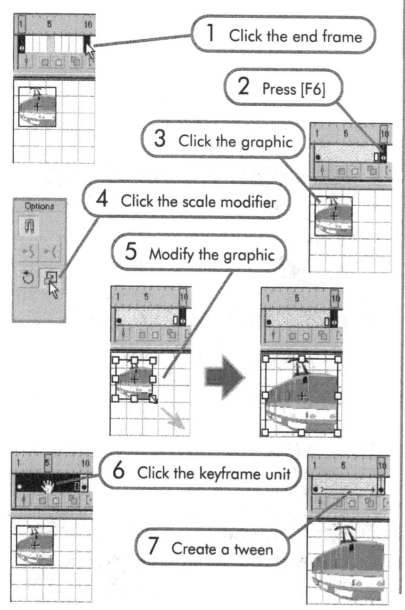

1 Click the end frame

2 Press [F6]

3 Click the graphic

4 Click the scale modifier

5 Modify the graphic

6 Click the keyframe unit

7 Create a tween

1 Click on an end frame for the motion tween.

2 Press [F6] to insert a keyframe at the chosen frame.

3 Click on the graphic to ensure it is selected.

4 Click the scale button in the toolbox options panel.

5 Click and drag the handles to resize the graphic. Drag the graphic itself to reposition it on the stage.

6 Click any frame in the keyframe unit.

7 Right-click and choose Create Motion Tween on the context menu.

☐ Flash creates a motion tween that changes the graphic's size in gradual steps from its start to end size.

☐ The new motion tween animation can be previewed by pressing [Enter].

100

Basic steps

1 With a symbol on the stage, click on an end frame for the tween.

2 Press [F6] to insert a keyframe at the selected point.

3 Click Window > Panels > Effect on the toolbar to launch the Effect window.

4 Click the button to display the menu.

5 Click the property you want to change – choose the Tint option to change the colour.

6 Click the colour that you want the graphic to become.

7 Click any frame in the keyframe unit.

8 Right-click and choose Create Motion Tween on the context menu.

❑ Flash creates a motion tween that changes the graphic colour in gradual steps from its start to end colour.

Tweening colour

Tweening can automatically generate intermediate frames for changes to the colour, or transparency, of a symbol instance. This can be used to fade a graphic in and out, or to fade a graphic from one colour to another.

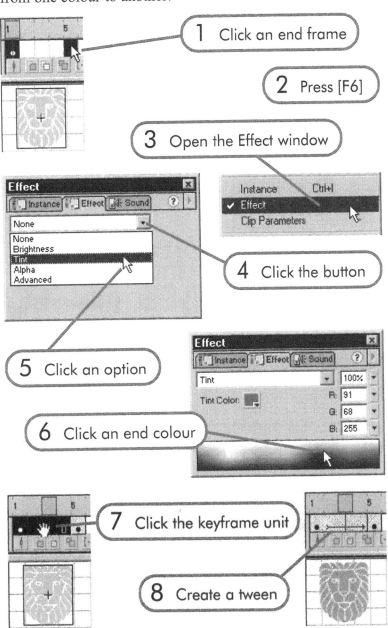

1 Click an end frame

2 Press [F6]

3 Open the Effect window

4 Click the button

5 Click an option

6 Click an end colour

7 Click the keyframe unit

8 Create a tween

Tweening rotation

Motion tweening can automatically generate intermediate frames for changes to the orientation of a graphic. This can be used to rotate a graphic or make a spinning graphic. As with other motion tweens, Flash calculates the difference between two keyframes to generate the images in the in-between frames. By default the direction of rotation will automatically be that which requires the shortest amount of rotation.

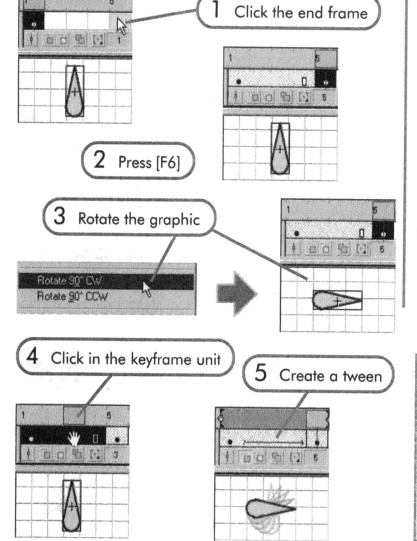

1 Click the end frame

2 Press [F6]

3 Rotate the graphic

Rotate 90° CW
Rotate 90° CCW

4 Click in the keyframe unit

5 Create a tween

Basic steps

1 With a symbol on the stage, click on an end frame for the tween.

2 Press [F6] to insert a keyframe at the selected point.

3 Click Transform – Rotate 90° CW in the Modify menu options to rotate the graphic 90° clockwise.

4 Click any frame in the keyframe unit.

5 Right-click and choose Create Motion Tween on the context menu.

❑ Flash creates intermediate steps that will rotate the graphic 90 degrees clockwise.

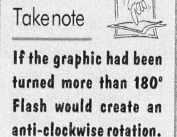

Take note

If the graphic had been turned more than 180° Flash would create an anti-clockwise rotation.

Setting rotation properties

Basic steps

1 With a symbol on the stage, click on an end frame for the tween.

2 Press [F6] to insert a keyframe at the selected point.

3 Click any frame in the keyframe unit.

4 Right-click and choose Create Motion Tween on the context menu.

5 Press [Ctrl+F] to open the Frame dialog box.

6 Choose a rotation direction from the drop-down menu and enter the total number of rotations desired.

❑ Flash creates a motion tween calculated from the specified direction and number of spins – in this example the graphic will make two clockwise rotations.

❑ You can preview this animation by pressing [Enter].

The default direction of rotation is not always the one that is required. For instance, you may want Flash to rotate the example on the facing page in an anti-clockwise direction. The direction of rotation can be specified manually in the Frames dialog box. The total number of rotations can also be specified here. This can be used to create a graphic that spins a set number of times in a specified direction.

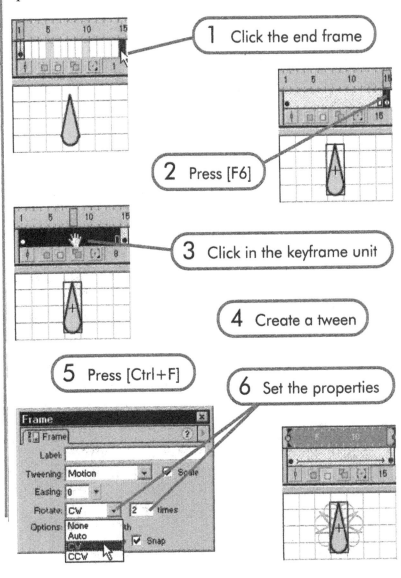

1 Click the end frame

2 Press [F6]

3 Click in the keyframe unit

4 Create a tween

5 Press [Ctrl+F]

6 Set the properties

Shape tweening

Flash can create intermediate frames between shapes on two keyframes using shape tweening. This is similar to motion tweening but with one important difference – motion tweening only works with symbols whereas shape tweening only works with editable graphics. To specify shape tweening choose the Shape option from the Tweening menu in the Frame dialog box.

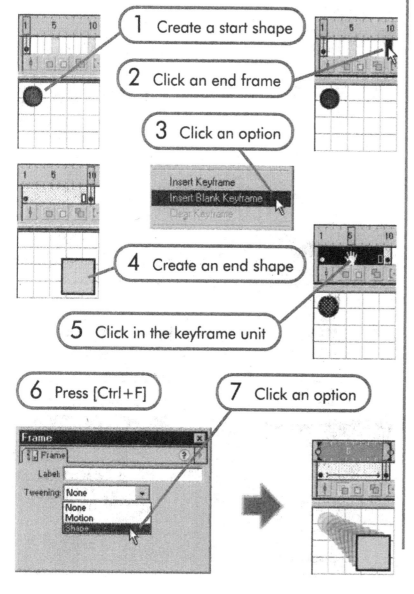

Basic steps

1 Create the starting shape on the stage.

2 Click on an end frame for the shape tween.

3 Right-click and choose Insert Blank Keyframe on the context menu.

4 Create the end shape on the stage.

5 Click any frame in the keyframe unit.

6 Press [Ctrl+F] to open the Frame dialog box.

7 Click the button to open the drop-down menu, then choose the Shape option.

❑ Flash creates a shape tween that changes the graphic's shape in gradual steps from its start to end shape.

❑ The tween also steps the shape's colours and its position.

❑ You can preview this animation by pressing [Enter].

Motion guide layers

Basic steps

1 Click on the layer to be associated then click the Add Guide Layer icon – in this example the Ball layer contains a 10-frame motion tween.

2 Click the pencil tool icon in the toolbox.

3 Draw the desired path on the stage.

4 Drag the graphic in each keyframe so that every centre point is aligned on the path.

❑ The path drawn in the motion guide layer will be followed by each frame in the associated layer.

❑ The path line does not appear in the final movie.

❑ You can test this movie animation by pressing [Ctrl+Enter].

A motion guide layer is a special layer that only contains a path along which to animate a graphic in an associated normal layer. To create a motion guide layer click on the layer that is to be associated then click the Add Guide Layer icon. The pencil tool can now be used to draw the desired path in the motion guide layer. Once the centres of the graphic in the start and end keyframes are aligned with the guide the animation will travel along the prescribed path.

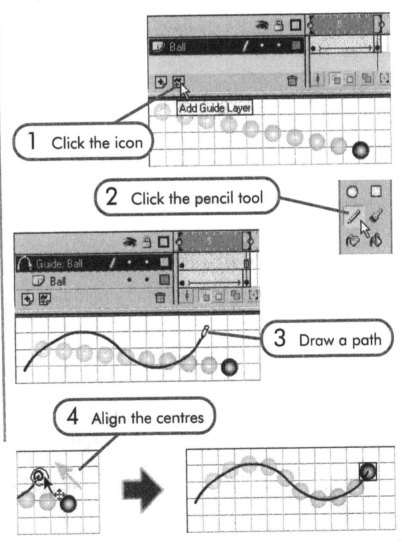

1 Click the icon

2 Click the pencil tool

3 Draw a path

4 Align the centres

Orienting to a path direction

Animations that follow a path on a motion guide layer may seem to be a little unnatural if they maintain a fixed orientation. For instance, an aeroplane flying a loop-the-loop should at some point be upside down, and not maintain a horizontal position. We can make the graphic follow the path more naturally by ticking the Orient to path option in the Frame dialog box. It is also better to rotate the graphic in the first keyframe to face in the direction of the path so that the initial alignment is natural.

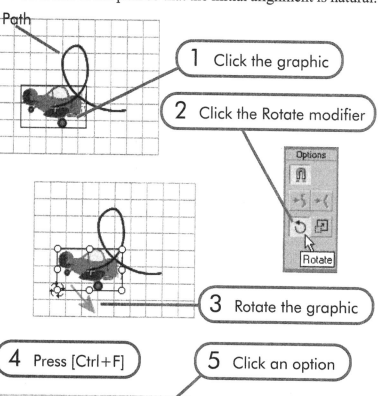

Path

1 Click the graphic

2 Click the Rotate modifier

Options

Rotate

3 Rotate the graphic

4 Press [Ctrl+F]

5 Click an option

Frame

Frame

Label:

Tweening: Motion ▾ ☑ Scale

Easing: 0 ▾

Rotate: Auto ▾ 0 times

Options: ☑ Orient to path
☑ Synchronize ☑ Snap

1 Click on the graphic in the first keyframe of the motion tween.

2 Click the Rotate modifier in the toolbox Options panel.

3 Drag the handles to align the graphic in the direction of the motion path

4 Press [Ctrl+F] to open the Frame dialog box.

5 Click on the box to tick the Orient to path option in the dialog.

❑ The graphic is now oriented to the path during the animation.

Tip

To manually adjust the orientation of an in-between frame right-click it and select Insert Keyframe, then rotate the graphic.

Basic steps

1 Press [Ctrl+F] to open the Frame dialog box.

2 Click on the arrowed button next to the Easing option field.

3 Drag the slider down to a negative value to set an Easing In effect.

❏ The word In appears alongside the slider.

Or

4 Drag the slider up to a positive value to set an Easing Out effect.

❏ The word Out appears alongside the slider.

❏ The speed of the animation will now vary in accordance with the Easing value.

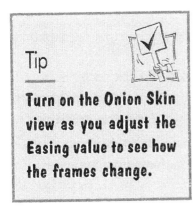

Tip

Turn on the Onion Skin view as you adjust the Easing value to see how the frames change.

Adjusting tween speed

Animations that are created using tweening spread the motion evenly across the total number of in-between frames in that sequence. The speed of a tweened animation cannot therefore be changed by adjusting the number of frames in the sequence as we did with the frame-by-frame animation example on page 93. Instead tweened animation speeds can be varied by setting the Easing value in the Frame dialog box. This value is zero by default when the frame rate is constant. Changing this to a negative value makes the animation start slowly then accelerate. This is called Easing In. A positive value on the other hand produces an Easing Out effect where the animation starts quickly then decelerates.

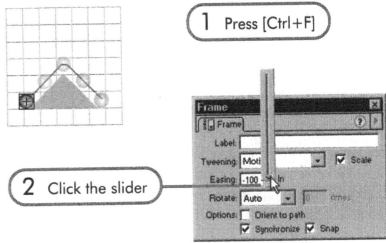

1 Press [Ctrl+F]

2 Click the slider

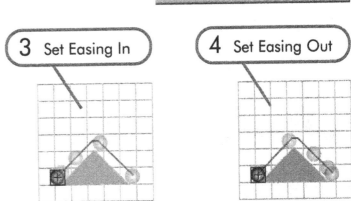

3 Set Easing In

4 Set Easing Out

Multiple motion tweens

Multiple items can be tweened simultaneously if they are each placed on their own layer. This is especially useful for animating characters, by placing separate parts on individual layers, to avoid repeatedly re-creating the entire character. Onion Skin view can be used to ensure that the parts align correctly.

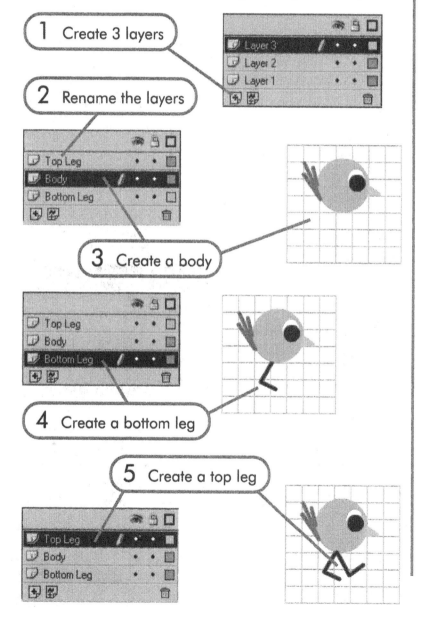

1 Create 3 layers

2 Rename the layers

3 Create a body

4 Create a bottom leg

5 Create a top leg

1 Click the Add Layer button twice to create a total of 3 layers for multiple tweening.

2 Click on each layer's label and rename it with meaningful names for its content.

3 Click on the Body layer and create a character body on the stage.

❑ The body will form part of the character although it will not be animated itself.

4 Click on the Bottom Leg layer and add a leg to the character on the stage.

5 Click on the Top Leg layer and add another leg to the character on the stage.

❑ The character is now completed on 3 layers and is ready to be animated by motion tweening the layers.

6 Hold down [Shift] and click an end frame for each layer. Release [Shift] then press [F6] to insert a keyframe in each one.

7 Hold down [Shift] and click each keyframe unit. Release [Shift] then right-click and choose Create Motion Tween from the context menu.

8 Click on the end frame in the Bottom Leg layer then move the bottom leg to its end position on the stage.

9 Click on the end frame in the Top Leg layer then move the top leg to its end position on the stage.

❑ The animated character is now complete and can be previewed by pressing [Enter].

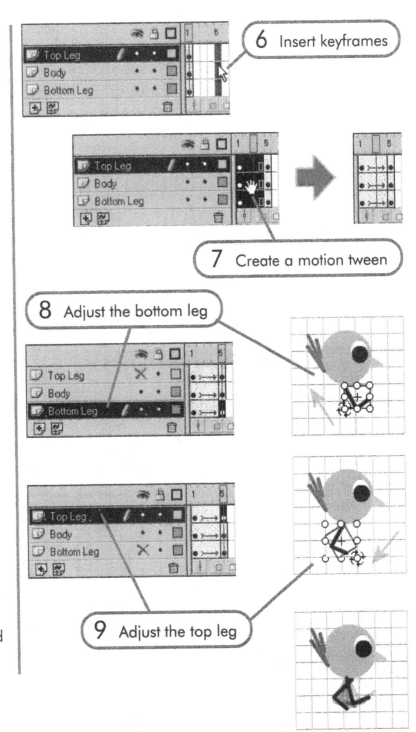

6 Insert keyframes

7 Create a motion tween

8 Adjust the bottom leg

9 Adjust the top leg

Movie Clip symbols

A complete multiple-frame, multiple-layer animated graphic can be stored in the Flash library as a Movie Clip symbol. This allows the animation to be reused, as often as desired, in other movies. Building a range of animated and static symbols enables you to make Flash movies that really come alive.

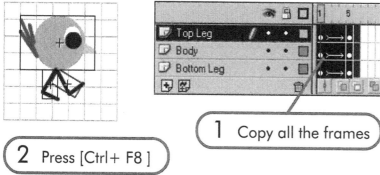

1 Copy all the frames

2 Press [Ctrl+ F8]

3 Type the name

4 Paste the frames

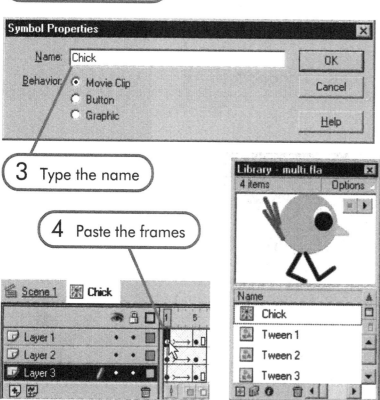

1 Select all frames on every layer of the animation then right-click and choose the Copy Frames option on the context menu.

2 Press [Ctrl+F8] to open the Symbol Properties dialog box.

❑ The Symbol Properties dialog box will open with the Movie Clip option selected.

3 Type a name for the new Movie Clip symbol in the name field then click [OK]

❑ Flash enters Editing Mode for this new symbol.

4 Click the first frame in the timeline then right-click and choose Paste Frames from the context menu.

❑ You can now access the new symbol from by pressing [Ctrl+L] to open the library.

Using Movie Clip symbols

1 Click File > Open as Library, or just press [Ctrl+Shift+O] then open the file that contains the symbol you want to use.

❏ The library window opens showing the symbols in that file.

2 Click on the desired symbol and drag an instance of it from the library onto the stage.

3 Click on an end frame for the tween then right-click and choose Insert Keyframe

4 Click on any frame in the keyframe unit then right-click and choose Create Motion Tween on the context menu.

❏ The graphic will now animate as it moves along the tween.

❏ Preview does not give the full effect – to see the full animation press [Ctrl+Enter].

All types of symbols that are stored in any Flash library can be made available to add to the current movie. You can add an animated graphic that is stored as a Movie Clip symbol then further animate it with a new tween. This is useful to make a walking-on-the-spot animated character move around the movie.

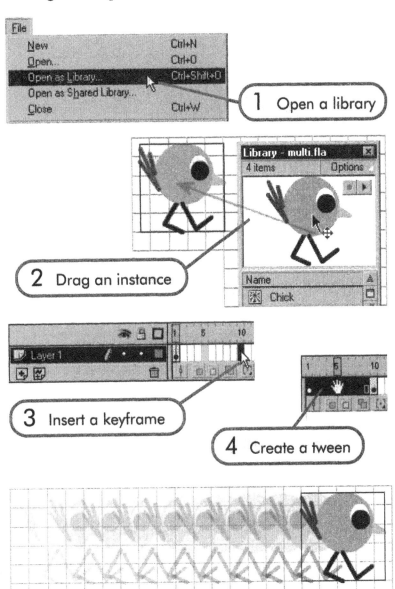

1 Open a library

2 Drag an instance

3 Insert a keyframe

4 Create a tween

Summary

❑ Motion tweening generates the in-between frame steps for movement of a graphic around a movie.

❑ A motion tween can be created using the Create Motion Tween option on the timeline context menu.

❑ A motion tween can also be created by setting the Tweening property in the Frame dialog box.

❑ Motion tweening can be used to animate the position, size, colour and orientation of a graphic.

❑ Shape tweening can be used to create the intermediate steps between graphics in two keyframes.

❑ The desired direction of a rotating animation can be specified in the Frame dialog box.

❑ Motion tweening works only with graphics whereas shape tweening works only with editable graphics.

❑ A motion guide layer can specify the path along which an animated graphic will travel.

❑ The tween speed can be adjusted by setting the Easing property in the Frame dialog box.

❑ Multiple items can be tweened simultaneously if they are each placed on their own layer.

❑ Complete animated graphics can be stored in a Flash library as a Movie Clip symbol.

❑ Any Flash file can be opened as a library to make its symbols available for use in the current movie.

10 Interactive buttons

Rollover buttons

Buttons can be included in Flash to allow the user to interact directly with a movie. The visual appearance of an interactive button should change as the user places the cursor over the button, or clicks on the button, to provide feedback. This is called a rollover effect. In Flash a special type of button symbol automatically provides four frames labelled Up, Over, Down and Hit in which slightly different button graphics can be stored to represent each stage of the rollover effect.

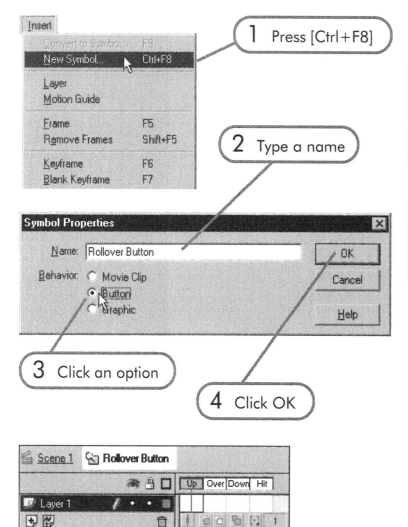

1 Press [Ctrl+F8]

2 Type a name

3 Click an option

4 Click OK

1 Press [Ctrl+F8], or select New Symbol on the toolbar Insert menu, to open the Symbol Properties dialog box.

2 Type a name for the new button symbol.

3 Click the Button option to specify that the new symbol will be an interactive button.

4 Click OK.

❑ Flash creates a new symbol in the library.

❑ The stage enters edit mode with frames shown on the timeline for each button state.

Basic steps

1 With the button symbol in edit mode click on the first frame in the button's timeline.

2 Create a graphic on the stage that will represent the button in its natural Up state.

3 Click the second frame then right-click and choose Insert Keyframe from the context menu.

4 Create a graphic to represent the button in its Over state.

5 Click the third frame then right-click and click Insert Keyframe.

6 Create a graphic to represent the button in its Down state.

❑ The button now has an individual graphic associated with each of its rollover states.

Adding button graphics

The natural Up state of a rollover button displays the graphic that is held in the first frame of the button symbol's timeline. When the user places the cursor over a button the Over state displays the graphic held in the second frame of its timeline. A button's Down state displays the graphic in the third frame of the timeline when the user clicks the button. Each of these graphics can be added to the appropriate timeline frame when the button symbol is in edit mode on the stage.

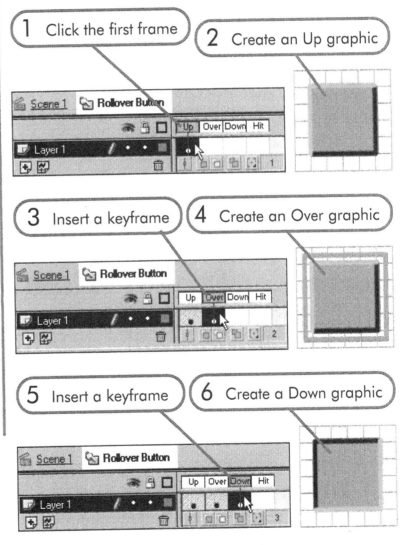

1 Click the first frame

2 Create an Up graphic

3 Insert a keyframe

4 Create an Over graphic

5 Insert a keyframe

6 Create a Down graphic

Button Hit state

The fourth and final frame in the timeline of a button symbol is the Hit state that defines the active area of the button. For a typical graphical button this will simply be a block covering the same size as the graphics in the Up, Over and Down states. If the button is more complex, such as a piece of text or a line drawing, the block should cover the entire area of the button to avoid creating any unresponsive spots. The Hit frame's contents are never actually displayed so they need only be a single-colour block defining the active button area.

1 Click the fourth frame on the timeline then right-click and choose Insert Keyframe from the context menu.

❑ The graphics from the Down keyframe are now copied to the Hit keyframe.

2 Use the paint bucket tool to fill the area with one solid colour.

3 Press [Ctrl+E] to return the stage to normal mode.

4 Press [Ctrl+L] to open the movie's library window.

❑ The library window shows the completed button symbol.

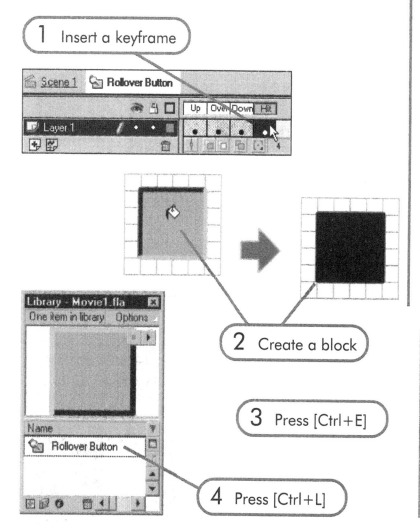

1 Insert a keyframe

2 Create a block

3 Press [Ctrl+E]

4 Press [Ctrl+L]

Tip

Press the play button in the library view to preview the Up, Over, Down and Hit frames.

Basic steps

1 Drag an instance of a library button symbol onto the stage.

2 Press [Ctrl+Alt+B] or select Control > Enable Simple Buttons from the toolbar.

3 Put the cursor over the button to test the button's Over state.

4 Click on the button to test its Down state.

Button preview

The rollover effects of a button are not usually enabled in normal editing mode. This allows the button to be repositioned on the stage without encountering the various button states. A button can, however, be previewed in normal editing mode by switching on a feature called Enable Simple Buttons. This is an option found on the toolbar's Control menu, or just press [Ctrl+Alt+B]. Alternatively the rollover effects can be seen in Test Movie mode by pressing [Ctrl+Enter].

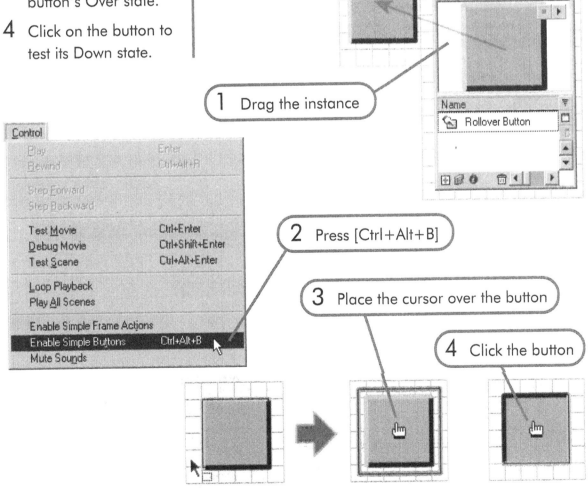

1 Drag the instance

2 Press [Ctrl+Alt+B]

3 Place the cursor over the button

4 Click the button

117

Adding button actions

To make a button actually do something when the user clicks it requires an action to be added to the button. Actions can be added to frames and objects, such as a button, using the Flash ActionScript scripting language. Learning ActionScript means learning a new language and is beyond the scope of this book. We can, however, get a taste of ActionScript by exploring how actions can be added to rollover buttons. A typical use for a button might be to relocate to another frame when it is clicked. Similarly, the new location might also have a button to return to the original location when the user clicks it.

Basic steps

1 Create 2 frames, each with a rollover button.

❑ First add actions to stop the frames from playing automatically.

2 Select frame 1.

3 Press [Ctrl+Alt+A] or click the Show Actions button to open the Actions dialog box.

4 Click the + button to see the Actions menu.

5 Click the Stop option – then repeat the same process for frame 2.

❑ Both Stop actions are added in the timeline.

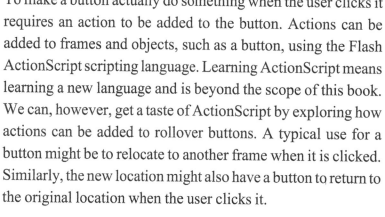

1 Create two frames

2 Click on frame 1

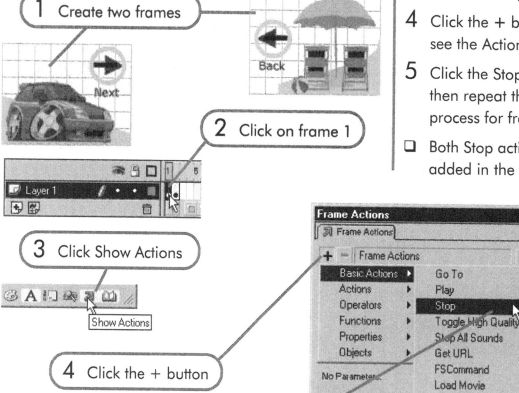

3 Click Show Actions

Show Actions

4 Click the + button

5 Click the Stop option

- ❏ Now add actions for each button to relocate the frame when the button is clicked.

6 First select the rollover button on the stage for frame 1.

- ❏ The actions dialog box automatically changes from Frame Actions to Object Actions

7 Click the + button to see the Actions menu.

8 Click on the Go To menu option.

- ❏ ActionScript code that will execute the relocation appears in the Actions window.

9 Type the number of the destination frame in the Frame field – then repeat the same process for frame 2.

- ❏ Responsive actions are now added to both buttons. To try the actions in test mode, press [Ctrl+Enter].

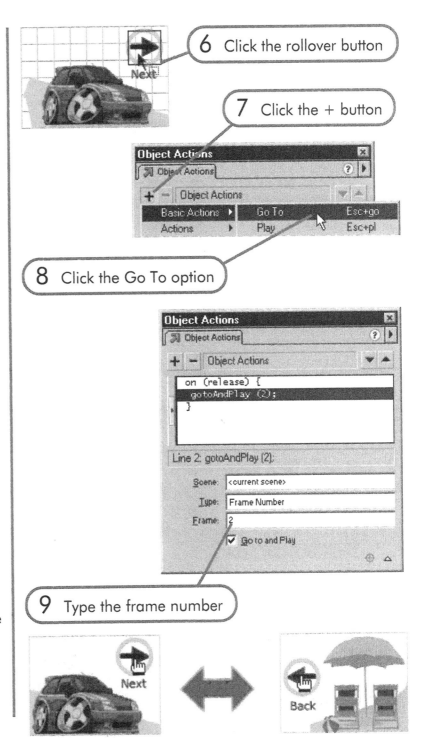

6 Click the rollover button

7 Click the + button

8 Click the Go To option

9 Type the frame number

119

Invisible buttons

The only button frame that must have a graphic is the Hit frame that defines the active area of the button. Buttons that do not have graphics in the Up, Over and Down frames will be invisible in the movie. An invisible button can be used to make the entire movie frame clickable. This is useful to resume playback of a movie that pauses on a frame containing a lot of text.

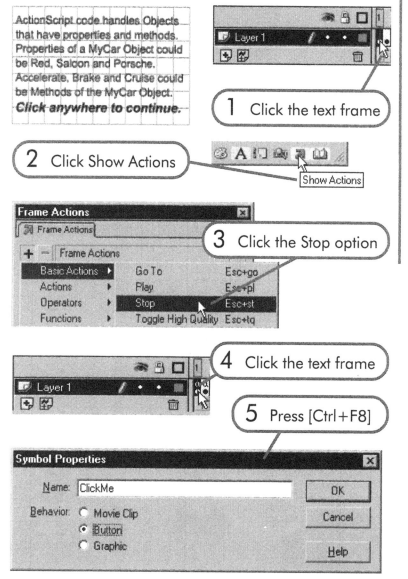

1 Click the text frame

2 Click Show Actions

Show Actions

3 Click the Stop option

4 Click the text frame

5 Press [Ctrl+F8]

1 Click on the keyframe with a lot of text.

2 Press [Ctrl+Alt+A] or click on the Show Actions button.

3 Add a Stop action to the first keyframe then repeat the process for the next keyframe.

4 Click on the keyframe with a lot of text.

5 Press [Ctrl+F8] to open the new Symbol Properties dialog box. Type a name, select the Button option then click OK to finish.

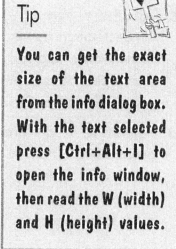

Tip

You can get the exact size of the text area from the info dialog box. With the text selected press [Ctrl+Alt+I] to open the info window, then read the W (width) and H (height) values.

6 Right-click the Hit frame then choose the Insert Blank Keyframe context menu option.

7 On the stage draw a box the same size as the text block – this button is now added to the library.

8 Press [Ctrl+E] to return to normal editing mode then press [Ctrl+L] to open the library.

9 Drag an instance of the invisible button from the library and position it exactly over the text block.

❑ Flash displays a transparent version of the Hit frame graphic.

10 With the invisible button selected press [Ctrl+Alt+A] and add a Play action.

❑ The entire text area is now active and the user may click it to advance the movie.

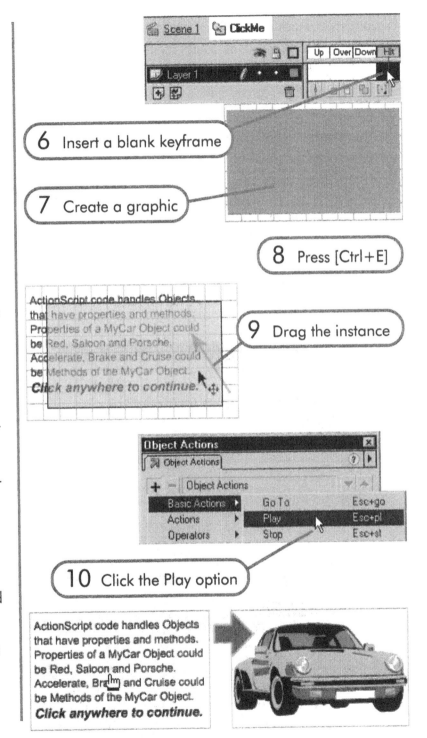

6 Insert a blank keyframe

7 Create a graphic

8 Press [Ctrl+E]

ActionScript code handles Objects that have properties and methods. Properties of a MyCar Object could be Red, Saloon and Porsche. Accelerate, Brake and Cruise could be Methods of the MyCar Object. **Click anywhere to continue.**

9 Drag the instance

Object Actions

Object Actions

+ − Object Actions

Basic Actions ▶ Go To   Esc+go
Actions ▶   Play   Esc+pl
Operators ▶   Stop   Esc+st

10 Click the Play option

ActionScript code handles Objects that have properties and methods. Properties of a MyCar Object could be Red, Saloon and Porsche. Accelerate, Brake and Cruise could be Methods of the MyCar Object. **Click anywhere to continue.**

Creating hot spots

Invisible buttons can be used to create hot spots in the movie frame that will respond to the user's mouse movements. The graphic in the button's Hit frame does not need to correspond to any other graphic so can be made any shape and size to create a hot spot anywhere in the frame. Several hot spots could be added to a single existing graphic if they do not overlap. The hot spot can respond to a mouse click by adding content to its Down frame. The Over frame can create a pop-up effect when the user's mouse is placed over the hot spot.

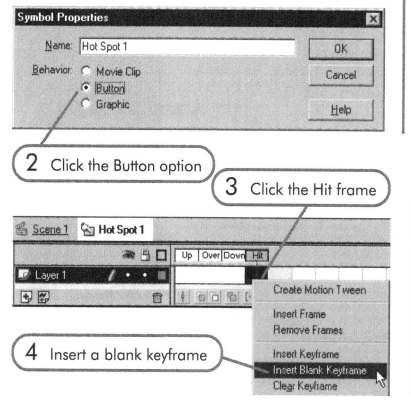

1 Press [Ctrl+F8]

2 Click the Button option

3 Click the Hit frame

4 Insert a blank keyframe

1 Press [Ctrl+F8] to open the Symbol Properties dialog box.

2 Type a name for the new symbol in the Name field and click the Button option then click OK.

❑ The stage enters edit mode with the new symbol name showing on the timeline.

3 Click the Hit frame to select it.

4 Right-click on the Hit frame to open the context menu then choose the Insert Blank Keyframe item.

Tip

Final adjustments can be made to the shape and size of the hot spot in normal mode with the arrow tool's scale and rotate modifiers.

5 Create a single-colour graphic on the stage to determine the shape and size of the hot spot.

6 Click the Over frame to select it.

7 Turn on Onion Skin view to see the Hit frame graphic then create a pop-up graphic on the stage.

8 Press [Ctrl+E] to return the stage to normal mode.

9 Press [Ctrl+L] to open the library window.

❏ The new symbol is listed in the library.

10 Drag an instance of the new symbol from the library and position the hot spot.

❏ The pop-up graphic will now appear whenever the mouse is over the hot spot.

❏ Press [Ctrl+Enter] to test the movie.

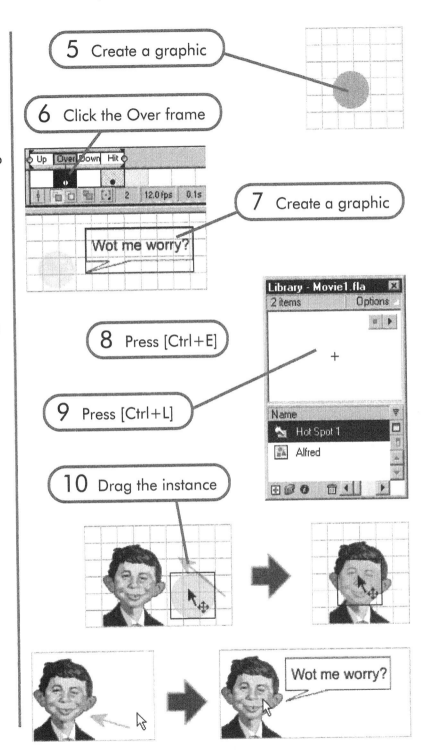

5 Create a graphic

6 Click the Over frame

7 Create a graphic

Wot me worry?

8 Press [Ctrl+E]

9 Press [Ctrl+L]

Library - Movie1.fla
2 items   Options
Name
Hot Spot 1
Alfred

10 Drag the instance

Wot me worry?

Summary

- A button allows the user to interact directly with a Flash movie.

- The button symbol automatically provides four frames labelled Up, Over, Down and Hit.

- An Up frame can contain a graphic that will be the natural state of the button.

- An Over frame can contain a graphic that will be the button's appearance when the mouse is placed over the button.

- A Down frame can contain a graphic that will be the appearance of the button when the user clicks it.

- The Hit frame must always contain a graphic that will define the shape and size of the button.

- Button actions can be previewed in normal editing mode with the Enable Simple Buttons feature.

- Actions can be added to frames or to objects using the Actions window.

- Adding Stop actions to frames will prevent the movie from playing all its frames automatically.

- The Play action will resume the movie and the Go To action can be used to relocate to another frame.

- A button symbol that has no graphics in its Up, Over and Down frames is an invisible button.

- An invisible button can be used to make the entire movie frame active.

- Hot spots can be incorporated into a frame by adding invisible buttons.

11 Adding sound

Importing sounds

Flash running on a Windows operating system can import sound files in WAV format and MP3 format for inclusion in a movie. These sound files are imported into Flash from the Import dialog box in just the same way as bitmaps or other artwork. The Import dialog box can be opened using the File > Import menu options or by pressing [Ctrl+R]. When a file is selected the sound is added as a new Symbol in that movie's Library.

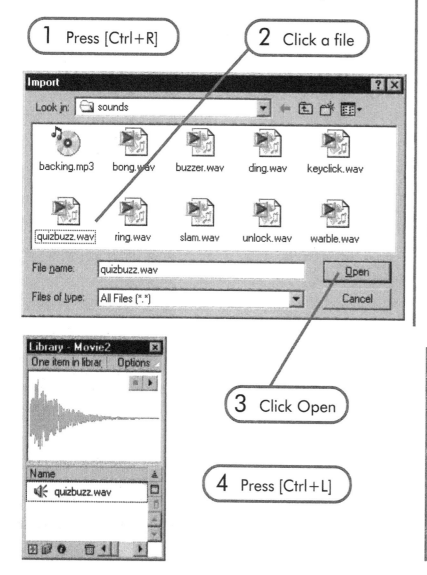

1 Press [Ctrl+R]

2 Click a file

3 Click Open

4 Press [Ctrl+L]

1 Click Import on the File menu or just press [Ctrl+R] to open the Import dialog box.

2 Navigate to the file to be imported and click on it to select it.

3 Click the Open button in the dialog box.

4 Press [Ctrl+L] to open the library.

❑ One or more instances of this sound symbol can now be added to the movie.

❑ To hear the sound select it in the library list then click the arrowed Play button in the library view.

Take note

If you have Quicktime 4 installed on your system you will also be able to import sound files in AIFF format.

Basic steps

1 Use the Add Layer button to make a new layer called Sounds

2 Press [Ctrl+L] to open the library.

3 With the Sounds layer selected drag an instance of a sound from the library onto the stage.

❏ The sound is attached to the first keyframe and its wave form graphic appears in the Sounds layer.

❏ Press [Ctrl+Enter] to test the movie sound.

As the number of components in a movie increases the timeline becomes increasingly cluttered. Although not essential it is a good idea to create a separate layer for actions and another separate layer for sounds so they can each be easily identified. Sounds can be attached to any keyframe by dragging an instance of the sound symbol from the library in the same way that other symbol instances are added to the movie. When a running movie reaches a keyframe that contains a sound that sound will begin to play then continue to the end of the sound clip regardless of the progress of the ensuing frames.

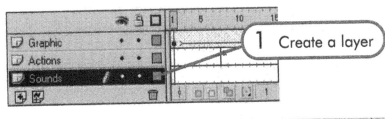

1 Create a layer

2 Press [Ctrl+L]

3 Drag the instance

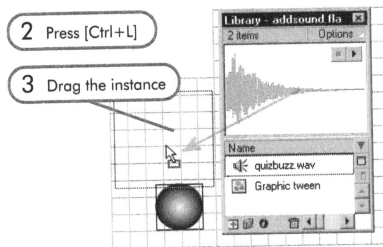

Take note

A Flash movie can have multiple sound layers.

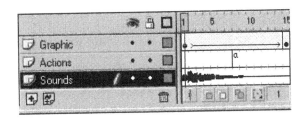

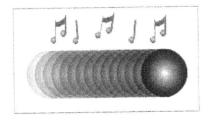

Button sound

Interactive buttons can be enhanced greatly by making the button produce a click sound when it is pushed by the user. This is easily achieved by adding a sound to the button's Down frame.

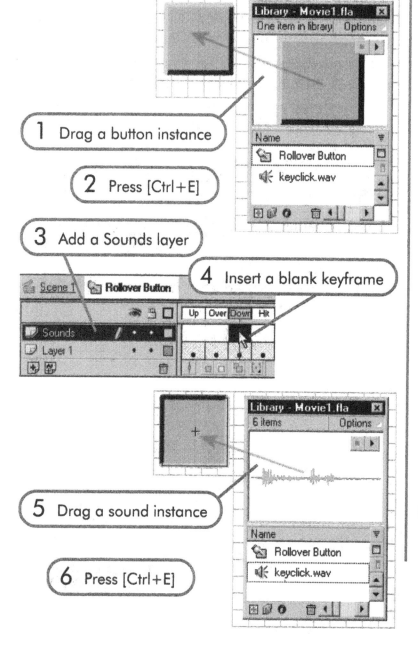

1 Drag a button instance

2 Press [Ctrl+E]

3 Add a Sounds layer

4 Insert a blank keyframe

5 Drag a sound instance

6 Press [Ctrl+E]

1 From the library, drag a button instance onto the stage.

2 Press [Ctrl+E] to open the button in Symbol-editing mode.

3 Add a new layer and name it Sounds

4 Right-click on the Down frame in the Sounds layer and choose Insert Blank Keyframe.

5 Drag a sound instance from the library onto the stage.

6 Press [Ctrl+E] to return to normal editing mode.

❑ The sound is attached to the Down frame of the button and will be played when the user pushes the button.

❑ Press [Ctrl+Enter] to try the button sound in test mode.

Basic steps

1 Click Window >
Panels > Sounds on
the toolbar or double-
click a frame to open
the Sound dialog box.

2 Click the Sound button
then choose a sound
from the drop-down
list, or use the current
selected sound.

3 Click the Effect button
then choose Fade Left
to Right from the
drop-down menu.

❑ Both the animation
and the sound move
from left to right when
the movie is played.

Take note

The Sound 2 layer in
this example does not
have a sound effect
added so will play nor-
mally, beginning when
the playhead reaches
frame 5 in the movie.

The Sound dialog box

Various sound properties can be controlled in the Sound dialog
box that can be opened by choosing Window > Panels > Sound
from the toolbar or by double-clicking on a frame in the timeline.
At the top of this dialog box is a drop-down list of all sounds in
the movie and details of the current selection are displayed. The
Sync property is set to Event by default to allow the sound to
play through once without synchronization with other frames.
The Effect field contains a drop-down menu of channel and fade
effects. It is useful to match a sound effect with an animation. For
instance you can match a graphic moving from left-to-right with
a sound that fades from the left speaker to the right speaker.

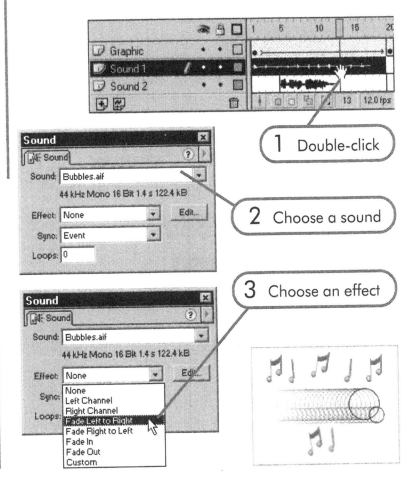

1 Double-click

2 Choose a sound

3 Choose an effect

Using Start sounds

Sounds that play normally have a Sync property set to Event. This Sync value can be changed in the Sound dialog box to Start, Stop or Stream to specify how the sound should be played. The Start setting is useful in looping movies to prevent accidentally playing multiple instances of a sound. Normally the default Event setting allows multiple instances of a sound to play concurrently but the Start setting will not play a sound if that sound is already playing.

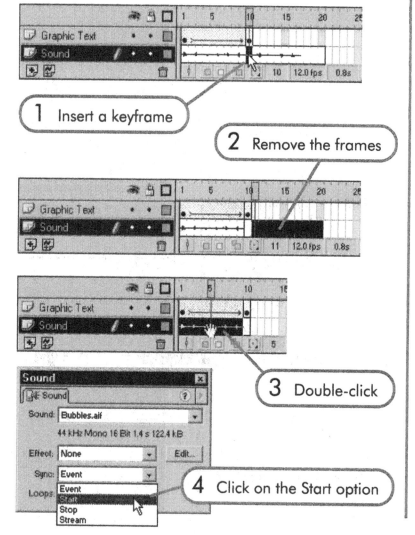

1 Insert a keyframe

2 Remove the frames

3 Double-click

4 Click on the Start option

Basic steps

1 Right-click on the frame in the Sound layer that is to be the end of the movie then choose the Insert Keyframe option from the context menu.

2 Drag the cursor over all frames after the new keyframe then press [Delete] to re-move them.

❑ When this movie plays in a loop the second iteration plays the end of the sound and a second instance of the sound begins to play.

3 Double-click the Sound layer keyframe unit to open the Sound dialog box.

4 Click the Sync button and choose the Start option from its menu.

❑ Now when this movie plays in a loop the second iteration plays only the end of the sound instance.

Basic steps

1 Right-click on the frame in the Sound layer where you want the sound to stop playing then choose Insert Blank Keyframe in the context menu.

2 Double-click the frame to open the Sound dialog box.

3 Click the Sound button and choose the sound to be stopped from the drop-down menu.

4 Click the Sync button and choose Stop from the drop-down menu.

5 Click anywhere on the stage to apply the new Stop setting.

❏ The waveform following the selected frame disappears and a filled square is placed in the frame to mark the end of the sound.

❏ When this movie is played the first sound no longer overlaps the second one.

Stopping sounds

Event sounds will normally play completely through but they can be made to stop prematurely by setting their Sync value to Stop in the Sound dialog box. Systems may play back sounds at different rates so it is useful to ensure that a sound has stopped before a new sound or action begins.

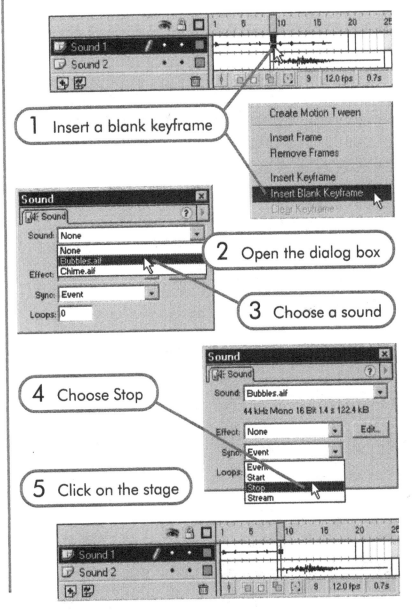

1 Insert a blank keyframe

2 Open the dialog box

3 Choose a sound

4 Choose Stop

5 Click on the stage

Streaming sounds

To avoid lengthy download delays of larger sound files when viewing Flash movies on the Internet, streaming sound allows the sound to start playing before the entire sound file has downloaded. When the Sync value of a sound is set to Stream, Flash breaks the sound into small clips that it synchronizes with frames in the movie. Each clip will be played when you scrub the playhead along the frames in the timeline. If the sound cannot fit into the number of frames available it will be truncated.

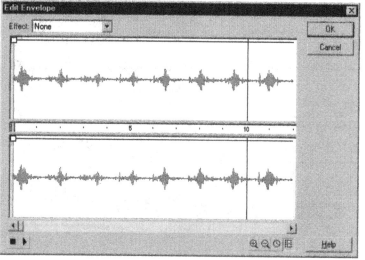

1 Double-click

3 Click Edit

2 Choose the Stream option

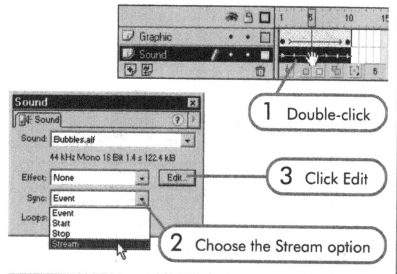

Basic steps

1 Double-click on the sound keyframe unit to open the Sound dialog box.

2 Click on the Sync button and choose the Stream option from the drop-down menu.

3 Click the Edit... button to open the Edit Envelope dialog box.

❏ The sound is broken into clips that are embedded in each frame of the movie.

❏ The Edit Envelope dialog box shows a line through the wave-form where the sound is truncated to fit into the available frames.

Tip

Drag the playhead along the timeline to hear each sound clip play.

Looping sounds

1   Double-click on the sound keyframe unit to open the Sound dialog box.

2   Click in the Loops field and replace the zero with the total number of times you want the sound to play.

3   Click anywhere on the stage to apply the new Loops setting.

❑   The sound will now repeat when the movie plays and the Sound layer shows a continuous waveform of all the sound loops.

❑   The Edit Envelope shows the repeated sounds greyed out.

A sound can be played repeatedly by setting the Loop value in the Sound dialog box with the number of times that the sound should repeat. Both Event sounds and Stream sounds can be looped this way. Flash combines the loops into a single continuous waveform. This means that a sound effect can be applied to the combined sound as if it were just a single sound. Any Sync setting will also be applied across all of the repeated sounds.

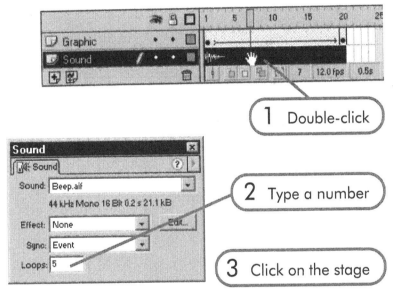

1   Double-click

2   Type a number

3   Click on the stage

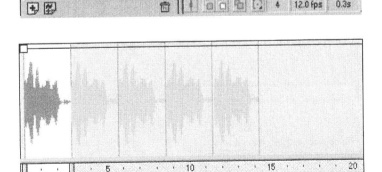

Tip

Loop a musical sound clip to add an efficient backing soundtrack to a movie.

Editing sounds

The Edit Envelope window allows a sound to be edited to change its volume or length, or to add custom effects. Waveform graphics are displayed in the Edit Envelope window for both left and right speaker channels. These are separated by a scale that can show either time in seconds or frame numbers. The choice of scale is toggled with the buttons at the bottom of this window. The scale also has two handles which denote the start and end of the sound. These can be dragged to new positions to remove part of the sound's beginning or end.

Basic steps

1 Double-click on the Sound keyframe unit to open the Sound dialog box.

2 Click on the Edit... button to open the Edit Envelope dialog box.

3 Click the Frames Scale button to show the waveform by frame numbers.

4 Drag the handle to omit the end of the sound.

5 Click OK to close the Edit Envelope dialog box then click on the stage to apply the new sound length.

❑ The sound is truncated to just 3 frames long.

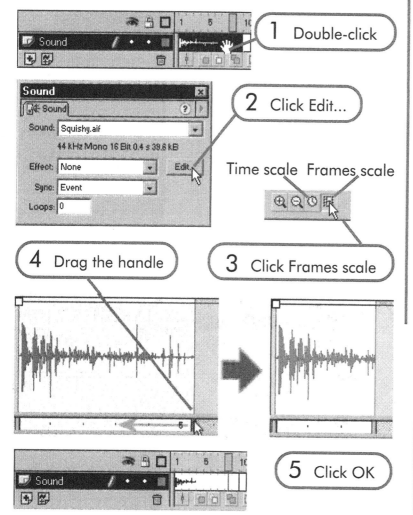

1 Double-click

2 Click Edit...

Time scale Frames scale

4 Drag the handle

3 Click Frames scale

5 Click OK

Take note

A movie still contains the full sound even if it has been edited.

Basic steps

1 Click the Effect button then choose Custom from the menu.

2 Click on the waveform to add handles.

3 Drag the handles to form the sound effect.

4 Click the OK button to close the Edit Envelope dialog box then click on the stage.

❑ The sound will gain the new custom effect.

Custom sound effects

The range of standard effects that are available in the Sounds dialog box can be modified in the Edit Envelope or new custom effects can be created. When the Custom option is selected a click on the waveform graphic will add new handles that can be dragged to adjust the volume level of each speaker in order to create a custom sound effect.

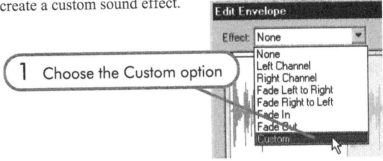

1 Choose the Custom option

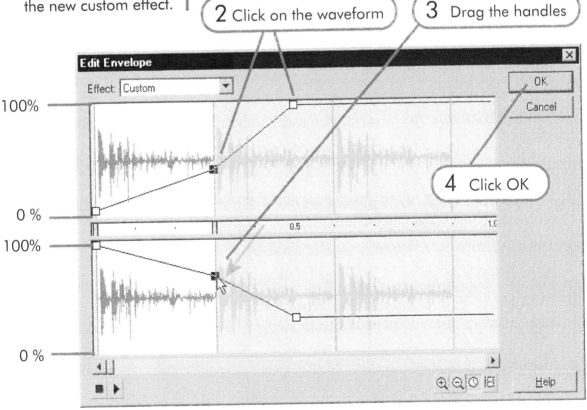

2 Click on the waveform

3 Drag the handles

4 Click OK

Summary

❑ Flash can import WAV and MP3 sound files for use in a movie.

❑ Imported sounds appear in the library view as a waveform graphic.

❑ A sound can be dragged from the library onto the stage to attach the sound to a keyframe.

❑ It is advisable to create a separate layer for sounds.

❑ Once started a sound will normally play to its end regardless of how the ensuing frames progress.

❑ Sounds can be added to a button state in Symbol-editing mode.

❑ The Sound dialog box provides a range of standard effects that can be applied to a sound.

❑ A Sync value of Event, Start, Stop or Stream can be specified in the Sound dialog box.

❑ A Start sound will only play if another instance of it is not already playing.

❑ A Stop instruction in the timeline will halt playback of a sound.

❑ Streaming breaks a sound into pieces that are then embedded into individual frames.

❑ A sound can be made to play several times by specifying a Loop value in the Sound dialog box.

❑ The Edit Envelope dialog box can be used to truncate sounds and create custom effects.

12 Delivering movies

Exporting from Flash

Flash can export a single frame or all the frames in a movie using the Export command options in the File menu. The currently selected frame can be exported using the Export Image option to a wide variety of formats including GIF, JPEG, BMP and Adobe Illustrator. The Export Movie option will export all frames in the movie as a sequence of sequentially numbered individual images in these formats. Additionally Export Movie can convert a Flash movie into a single animated GIF, a Windows AVI or a Quicktime MOV file.

1   Click File > Export Movie or press [Ctrl+Alt+Shift+S] to open the Export Movie dialog box.

2   Navigate to the desired destination then type a name for the new file.

3   Click the Save button to close the Export Movie dialog box.

❑   If an Export Options dialog box appears click OK to accept the default settings.

❑   A MOV file is created that can be played back with the Quicktime player.

1   Click on Export Movie

Import...	Ctrl+R
Export Movie...	Ctrl+Alt+Shift+S
Export Image...	
Publish Settings...	Ctrl+Shift+F12
Publish Preview	▶
Publish	Shift+F12

2   Type a name

3   Click Save

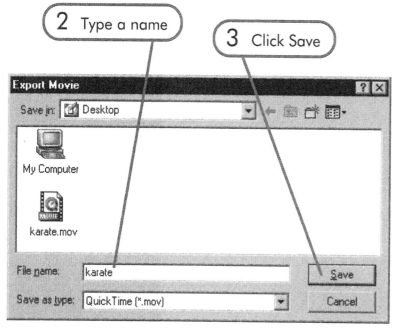

Export Movie

Save in: Desktop

My Computer

karate.mov

File name: karate

Save as type: QuickTime (*.mov)

Save

Cancel

karate.mov

Basic steps

1 Click File > Publish Settings or press [Ctrl+Shift+F12] to open the Publish Settings dialog box.

2 Select the Formats tab then on click the preferred platform.

3 Click the Publish button then click OK to close the Publish Settings dialog box.

❑ A Projector file is created in the same folder as the movie.

❑ You can double-click the Projector icon to play the movie.

Movie Projectors

A Flash movie can be made into a stand-alone application called a Projector. When a Projector file is executed it plays its movie automatically. This is a great way to deliver Flash movies directly, as e-mail attachments for instance. Projectors must be made to specifically suit either a Windows or a Macintosh operating system when they are created. This preferred platform is specified under the Formats tab of the Publish Settings dialog box that is available from the File menu. Once this has been set a simple click on the Publish button in the Publish Settings dialog box will create a Projector file in the same folder as the movie.

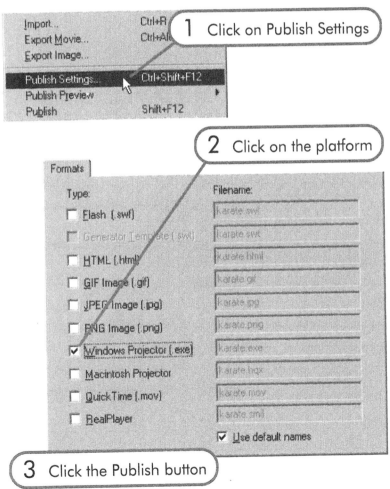

1 Click on Publish Settings

2 Click on the platform

3 Click the Publish button

139

Optimizing movies

Movies that are intended for delivery over the Internet should be kept to a small file size to prevent lengthy download delays. Some items that increase the movie file size include:

- Multiple bitmaps and animated bitmaps

- Embedded sound files and fonts

- Multiple keyframes instead of tweening

- Graphics that have gradient fills instead of one colour

- Separate graphic elements instead of symbols.

The Bandwidth Profiler in Test mode examines how a movie will download. This reveals frames that are likely to cause download delays so they can be amended to optimize the movie.

1 Press [Ctrl+Enter] to open test mode.

2 Click on the Debug menu then choose the desired modem speed for the test.

3 Click on the View menu then choose the Frame By Frame Graph menu option.

4 Click on the View menu then choose the Bandwidth Profiler menu option.

❑ The Bandwidth Profiler opens and displays a bar graph. Each bar represents the number of bytes of data in each frame.

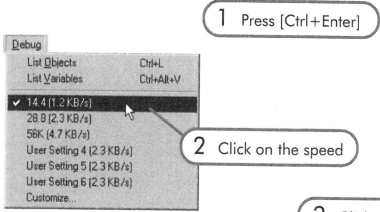

1 Press [Ctrl+Enter]

2 Click on the speed

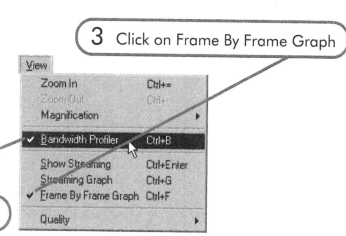

3 Click on Frame By Frame Graph

4 Click on Bandwidth Profiler

- ❏ The numbers on the top scale represent frame numbers and the bottom red line on the graph marks the frame data limit at the selected speed.

- ❏ Frames which exceed the limit (frame 1 and frame 11) may cause a download delay – examine ways to reduce their content size to avoid delays.

5 Click on the View menu and choose Streaming Graph.

6 Click on a frame bar to select that frame.

- ❏ The numbers on the top scale now represent units of time – for a 12-fps movie each one is 1/12 second.

- ❏ A single time unit can download several frames containing little data but a frame with lots of data may span several units.

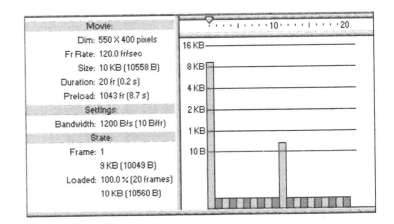

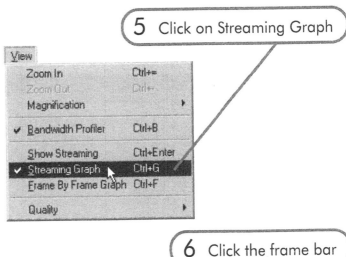

5 Click on Streaming Graph

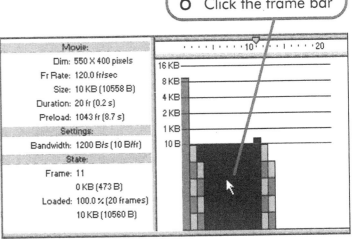

6 Click the frame bar

Publishing movies

Commonly Flash movies will be delivered on the Internet so the Publish command on the File menu can create the SWF movie file and also automatically generate a HTML file for the movie. This HTML document can then be opened in a Flash-enabled web browser to display the movie within an area on its page. Because Flash refers to its Publish Settings whenever the Publish command is used these must specify that both SWF and HTML files should be created on publication.

1 Click File > Publish Settings on the toolbar, or press [Ctrl+Shift+F12] to open the Publish Settings dialog box.

2 Click both the SWF and HTML options – deselect any others.

3 Click OK in the dialog box to apply the specified settings.

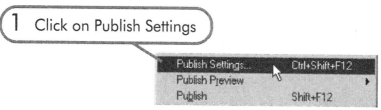

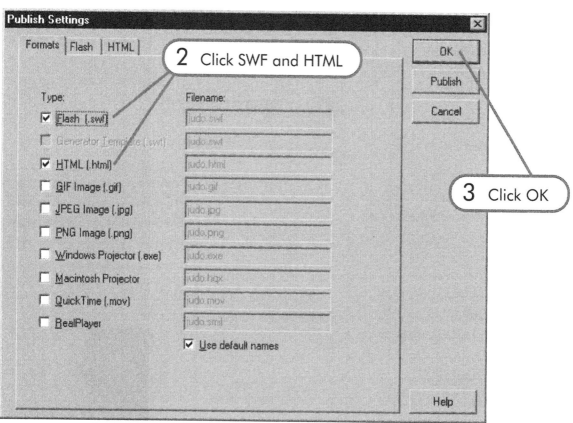

4 Click File > Publish on the toolbar, or press [Shift+F12] to generate the new files.

❑ The Publishing dialog box appears with a progress bar.

❑ On publication new HTML and SWF files are created in the same folder as the original FLA file.

5 Double-click the HTML file icon to open it in the system's default web browser.

❑ The Flash movie is now displayed in the browser window.

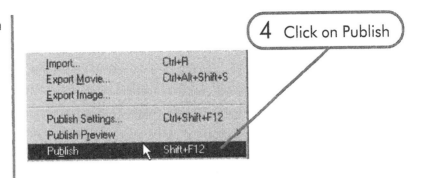

4 Click on Publish

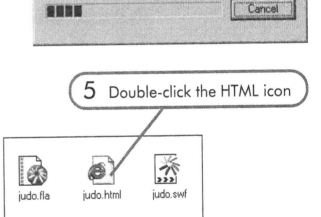

5 Double-click the HTML icon

judo.fla   judo.html   judo.swf

Tip

Use Publish Preview > HTML menu options to generate the files then automatically open the movie in the default web browser window.

Using HTML templates

The default Publish Settings that are used by Flash can be modified to suit your needs. Custom names can be given to the generated files and the HTML file can use a variety of templates. The default HTML template expects that the user's browser will have the Flash plugin installed but an alternative HTML file can be created that uses JavaScript to detect the browser and provide choices if the browser cannot display Flash movies.

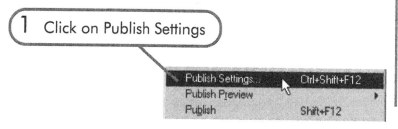

Basic steps

1 Click File > Publish Settings on the toolbar to open the Publish Settings dialog box.

2 Click the SWF, HTML and GIF options – deselect any others.

3 Uncheck the Use default names box and type new names.

4 Click the HTML tab.

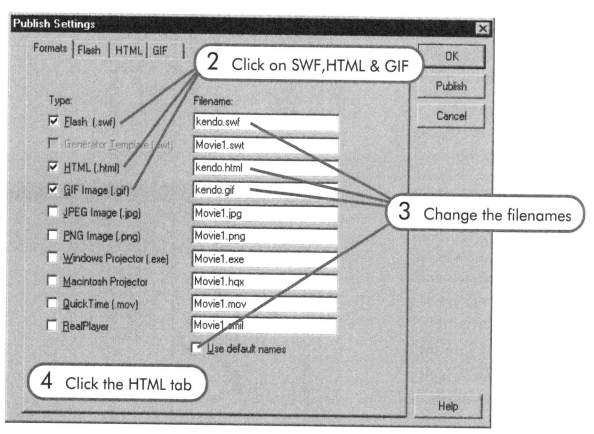

5 Click the Template button to open the drop-down list of standard templates.

6 Click on the User Choice option from the drop-down menu.

7 Click on the Publish button in the Publish Settings dialog box.

❑ Flash creates a SWF movie file in the same folder as the original FLA file.

❑ Flash generates a GIF image file from the movie's first frame.

❑ Flash also makes a HTML file containing JavaScript code. This will play the SWF file in browsers that have the Flash plugin or otherwise will display the GIF image file.

8 Open the generated HTML file in a browser to see the results.

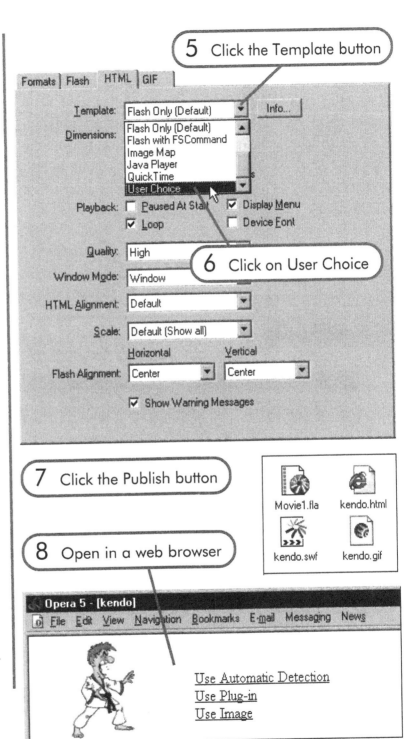

5 Click the Template button

6 Click on User Choice

7 Click the Publish button

8 Open in a web browser

Movie1.fla kendo.html

kendo.swf kendo.gif

Opera 5 - [kendo]
File   Edit   View   Navigation   Bookmarks   E-mail   Messaging   News

Use Automatic Detection
Use Plug-in
Use Image

145

Controlling dimensions

The original dimensions and background colour of a movie can be specified in the Movie Properties dialog box. When publishing for the Web, the area allocated for the movie on the web page will normally match these Movie Properties dimensions. Custom dimensions for this area can be specified in the HTML tab of the Publish Settings dialog box. This alone will not change the displayed size of the movie unless the Scale setting is also changed to 'Exact fit' for the specified area dimensions. This could be used to stretch a half-banner to full banner size.

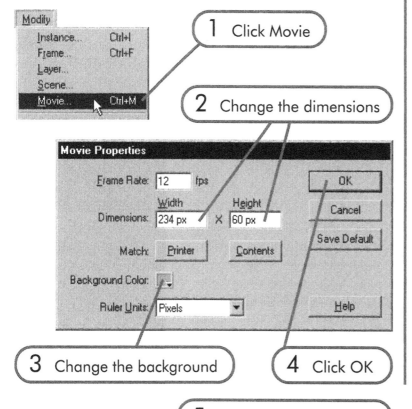

1 Click Movie

2 Change the dimensions

3 Change the background

4 Click OK

5 Click on Publish Settings

1 Click Modify > Movie or press [Ctrl+M] to open the Movie Properties dialog box.

2 Type the new desired movie dimensions in the Width and Height text fields.

3 Click on the colour block and choose a new background colour from the pop-up colour swatch.

4 Click the OK button to apply the new settings and close the Movie Properties dialog box.

❑ The Stage area changes to the new size and colour.

5 Click Publish Settings on the File menu or press [Ctrl+Shift+F12] to open the Publish Settings dialog box.

6 Select the HTML tab then click on the Dimensions button and choose Pixels from the menu.

7 Type the desired size into the Width and Height text fields.

8 Click the Scale button then choose the Exact fit option from the drop-down menu.

9 Click the Publish button to generate the specified files.

❑ Flash generates a SWF movie file to the original dimensions.

❑ Flash also creates a HTML file with the stated movie area and fits the movie to it.

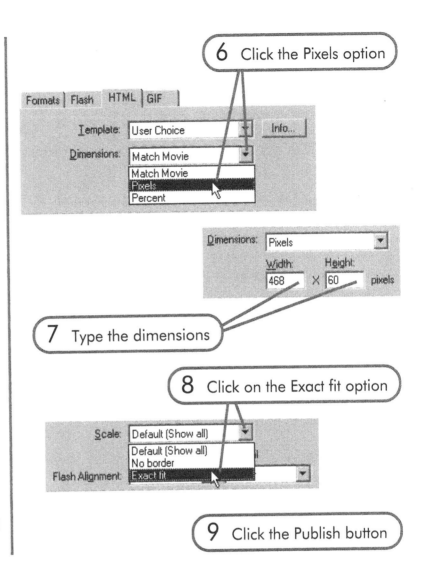

6 Click the Pixels option

7 Type the dimensions

8 Click on the Exact fit option

9 Click the Publish button

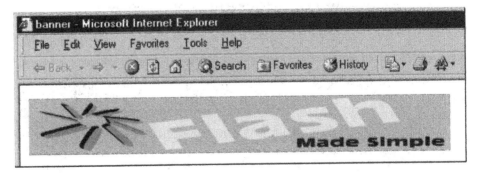

Summary

- ❏ Flash can export a single frame, or all frames in a movie, using the Export command in the File menu.

- ❏ Images can be exported in a variety of file formats including GIF, JPEG, BMP and Adobe Illustrator.

- ❏ Entire movies can be exported in a variety of formats including animated GIF, AVI and Quicktime.

- ❏ A Projector file is a stand-alone application that can be created by Flash to play a movie independently.

- ❏ The intended platform for a Projector file must be specified in the Format tab of the Publish Settings dialog box.

- ❏ Movies that are produced for delivery via the Web should be optimized to minimize download time.

- ❏ The Bandwidth Profiler can be used to discover items that may cause potential download delays.

- ❏ The Publish command is used to create a finished SWF movie file from the working FLA file.

- ❏ Flash can also generate HTML files whenever a finished movie is published.

- ❏ Using HTML templates can produce a HTML file with JavaScript code that will detect the Flash plugin.

- ❏ A movie's original size and background colour can be set in the Movie Properties dialog box.

- ❏ A movie's display area in a web page can be set in the HTML tab of the Publish Settings dialog box.

- ❏ The movie can be made to fit a specified page display area by setting its Scale to Exact fit.

Keyboard shortcuts

Keys	Function	Keys	Function
A	Select subselect tool	Ctrl+B	Break-apart a group into elements
B	Select the brush tool	Ctrl+D	Duplicate the selection
E	Select the eraser tool	Ctrl+E	Toggle symbol-editing mode
H	Select the hand tool	Ctrl+F	Open the Frame dialog box
I	Select eye dropper tool	Ctrl+G	Group the selected elements
K	Select paint bucket tool	Ctrl+I	Open the Instance dialog box
L	Select the lasso tool	Ctrl+L	Open the Library dialog box
N	Select the line tool	Ctrl+M	Open the Movie Properties dialog box
O	Select the oval tool	Ctrl+N	Open a new editor window
P	Select the pen tool	Ctrl+R	Open the Import dialog box
R	Select rectangle tool	Ctrl+T	Open the Text dialog box
S	Select ink bottle tool	Ctrl+Z	Undo the previous operation
T	Select the text tool	Ctrl+Enter	Test the movie
V	Select the arrow tool	Ctrl+Alt+A	Open the Actions dialog box
Y	Select the pencil tool	Ctrl+Alt+B	Enable simple buttons in the editor
Z	Select the zoom tool	Ctrl+Alt+I	Open the Info dialog box
F5	Insert a frame	Ctrl+Shift+A	Deselect all selected elements
F6	Insert a keyframe	Ctrl+Shift+G	Ungroup a graphic object
F7	Insert a blank keyframe	Ctrl+Shift+O	Open a Flash file as a library
F8	Convert to a symbol	Ctrl+Shift+V	Paste a clipboard in the original place
Ctrl+F8	Create a new symbol	Shift+F12	Publish files
Ctrl+#	Show/hide the grid	Ctrl+Shift+F12	Open the Publish Settings dialog box
Ctrl+A	Select all elements	Ctrl+Alt+Shift+S	Open the Export Movie dialog box

Index